BURN

and

ROSALIND

Deborah Gearing

BURN

and

ROSALIND

A QUESTION OF LIFE

OBERON BOOKS
LONDON

First published in this collection in 2006 by Oberon Books Ltd
521 Caledonian Road, London N7 9RH
Tel: 020 7607 3637 / Fax: 020 7607 3629
e-mail: info@oberonbooks.com
www.oberonbooks.com

PB ISBN: 978-1-84002-659-7
E ISBN: 978-1-84943-790-5

Visit www.oberonbooks.com to read more about all our books and to
buy them. You will also find features, author interviews and news of
any author events, and you can sign up for e-newsletters so that you're
always first to hear about our new releases.

Contents

BURN

Thanks to:

John Burgess, Nuffield Theatre Southampton, Kerry Angus, Raymond Elsner.

DG

Characters

SAL, Aaron's younger sister, 9

AARON, rhymes with 'Darren', also called Az, 15

SITA, 16

LINDA, 15

RACHEL, 16

BIRDMAN (Joey), 15

SOCIAL WORKER (Jan)

MEL, 16

MARIE, 16

TOM, 15

NIALL, 16

COLIN, 17

Set   About the stage is the debris which has been washed up by the river, as well as a fridge and some chairs, which may be used to make the car or indicate rooms as necessary.

A note on punctuation   A full stop denotes the end of a thought. A comma indicates a thought extending itself. A dash might be thought of as the suspension of a thought, a crystallisation.

Burn was originally part of the NT Shell Connections 2005 programme, and was first performed on 8 July 2005 at the Cottesloe, National Theatre, by Wired Youth Theatre, Northampton. It received its first professional production on 3 March 2006 at the Cottesloe, National Theatre, with the following company:

SAL, Alex Tregear
AARON, Robert Boulter
SITA, Farzana Dua Elahe
LINDA, Andrea Riseborough
RACHEL, Naomi Bentley
BIRDMAN, Andrew Garfield
SOCIAL WORKER, Joy Richardson
MEL, Claire-Louise Cordwell
MARIE, Matti Houghton
TOM, Matt Smith
NIALL, Sid Mitchell
COLIN, Javone Prince

Director, Anna Mackmin
Designer, Jonathan Fensom
Lighting Designer, Jason Taylor
Music, Paddy Cunneen
Sound Designer, Christopher Shutt
Production Manager, Laurence Holderness
Stage Manager, Clare Simmonds
Deputy Stage Manager, Tamara Albachari
Assistant Stage Managers, Cynthia Duberry
                                       Iain Farmery
Costume Supervisor, Jane Gooday
Publicists, Lucinda Morrison
              Pia de Souza

Scene One

A red glow.

SAL: Where are you starting?

AARON: At the beginning.

SITA: Birdman's story? It doesn't have a beginning.
It flows. It just all flows along this stretch of dirty water.

LINDA: Where are you starting?

AARON: On the way downriver.
Birdman went marching
down from the Manor and out towards the sea.

RACHEL: Where are you starting?

AARON: Early in the morning.
Birdman came to see me.
It was early in the morning
on that particular day.

The red glow fades to daylight.
Riverbank.
AARON, SAL loaded down with fishing rods and a plastic
bag, BIRDMAN.

AARON: Hear this.
Sea tang rising off the river.
I'm out of bed and down the stairs.
Birdman's waiting.
With his board.
Not boards, I say. Not today.
Smell that –
Birdman flaring his nostrils in the wind
like some beast.
Wolf.

Me and Sal, we're the pack.
But today I'm leading.
It's my shout.
(How Sal come to be part of this I don't want to tell –
tag-along, tell-tale, carry-all or I'll kick you down the bank.)
Come on, I say. Come on.
And we leave the Manor
heading for that white bridge that swoops
across the river.
Hogweed, cow parsley, rush, sedge, madder.
(Yeah, it's a girl thing, plants,
But I like the way they sound.)
I've got my stick
and a steady rhythm –
thwack, step, thwack, step, thwack.
Heads flying. Backs broken.
Smells – rank.
But we've got a steady pace –
I don't let up – sun's moving up
over the river.
Flies buzzing.
It's two miles down the river.
We're keeping step. Then.
Full stop.
Fence.
Railway line.
Sal
(sniveller, snot-maker, here blow it or I'll burn you to a
cinder).
Birdman. Me.

BIRDMAN: Leave her here.

AARON: Can't do that. C'mon Sal.

SAL: I can't do it. I can't do it. It's too dangerous. I said I wouldn't. I promised mum.

AARON: C'mon Sal. Just don't tread on the rails that's all.

SAL: I can't. I haven't got rubber shoes. I'm only wearing jellies.

AARON: They're rubber Sal. They'll be okay.

SAL: They're plastic stupid. Plastic's not the same as rubber.

AARON: You don't *have* to tread on the rails. Just don't tread on them. And you'll be okay.

SAL: I might touch the electric. By mistake.
And what if a train comes?

AARON: We'll hear it coming.

SAL: But what if I trip, and get caught up in something. I might fall on the line. Or the train will come and chop my head off.

AARON: Just shut up and get moving. Shut up.

He pushes her.

SAL: I can't. I can't do it. There was that boy.

AARON: What boy?

SAL: A boy from round here. Got killed on the line. They said.

AARON: Who said?

SAL: The police.

AARON: The police! When did you talk to the police?

SAL: At school. They came to visit.

AARON: That's just what they say. It's a show. They make it up to scare little kids. Like you.

SAL: No. It's true.

AARON: How do you know?
(*Pause.*)
How do you know?

SAL: They said so.
(*Beat.*)
She was all right the copper. She wouldn't make it up.

AARON: No? Well next time – you ask who it was. She won't be able to tell you. I guarantee. She'll say she can't tell you. And that's because she made it up. You can't ask them anything. They'll always lie. Now get through this hole and follow me.

SAL shakes her head.

BIRDMAN: Leave her here.

AARON: Can't do that.
Middle of nowhere.
No.
(*Pause.*)
Okay. Yes.
Sal. You come or you wait here. Up to you.

SAL: I'll stay here.

AARON: We'll be gone a long time.

SAL: I'm not coming. Leave me my sandwiches.

AARON: What if a dog comes?

SAL: I'll throw him my sandwiches.

AARON: Yeah?

SAL: I'll tell him to go away.

AARON: Yeah.

SAL: I'll scream.
(*Pause.*)
I think I'll go home. Now. Take me home.

AARON: Take you where? We've been walking for over half
an hour. We're heading down the river. You wait here or
you come with us. No – You come with us, or I'll knock
your head off. I'll take you down the allotments and
pass you round like Linda.
I shouldn't have said that.
That I shouldn't have said.
No one knows about the allotments except Linda. And
Sal and me, 'cos we found her. And the blokes who took
her there. She won't say who.
I shouldn't have said that.
Sal – supersonic. Really scared now.
Jelly in her jellies. Green in pink.
Pissing in her pants.
Birdman –

BIRDMAN: Gobshite. You gobshite. Talking to her like that.
She's your sister. You don't talk to her like that. Not
your sister.
Come on Sal.

SAL: Where are we going?

BIRDMAN: Taking you home.

SAL: What, my house?
Quickest way?

BIRDMAN: Quickest way is back the way we come.

SAL: What about the bus?

BIRDMAN: No money. You got any?

SAL: No.

BIRDMAN: Come on then. Walk.

AARON: What about the river?

BIRDMAN: Sod the river. Get her home. Why did you bring
her anyway?

AARON: Had to.

BIRDMAN: Had to? Do everything your mum says? Do you?

AARON: Get out of my face.
(*Beat.*)
You know she said I had to stay away from you.

Birdman goes quiet.
Picks up the pace.
In front.
Way in front.
Heading back up the river, back to the manor.
Through swarms of flies.

Scene Two

LINDA's house.
LINDA, with a dress shredded into strips.

LINDA: Hear this.
I shred that dress. The dress I wore that night. Long
strips. Red splashed on yellow. Mother came.
Ten fingers on my face.
Left. Right.
Red on yellow.
You're sick, mother said.
I might be.

And what's that mark on your arm?

Only half the mark I've got on my face mother.

Get to bed you cheeky mare. There's something wrong with you. Tearing up a good dress like that. Stinking out the place with Dettol. What do you do with it?

You're sick.

Yeah – sad-sick.

Mouse mouse in the house, shred herself a bed, lying in it, waiting for the sad-sickness to swell through her body.

Mother – and keep that door shut. Don't think you're going anywhere today.

Closing the door – There's something wrong with that girl.

Now see this.

(*Hiding the strips of cloth.*)

Midday. High sun.

Loud knocking at the door. Man's head in the circle of light.

From the top of the stairs:

Who is it?

From the foot of the stairs:

Whisper

Who is it?

Mouse mouse in the house

Eight and a half hours to dusk.

Who is it?

Boy's voice.

Boy not man.

Open up.

Jesus Christ Birdman. What are you doing here?

BIRDMAN: Dunno.

LINDA: What do you mean, you don't know?

BIRDMAN: Dunno. Just passing. I suppose. Thought I'd come round. See what you were doing.

LINDA: Well you've seen and you've been.

BIRDMAN: What are you doing?

LINDA: Just hanging.

BIRDMAN: You coming out?

LINDA: What with you?

BIRDMAN: Yeah. If you like.

LINDA: I'm busy.
   (*Beat.*)
   Where?

BIRDMAN: Park? I've got my board.

LINDA: I'm busy.

BIRDMAN: No you're not.

LINDA: I am.

BIRDMAN: You're just saying that.

LINDA: Well that means no, doesn't it?

BIRDMAN: Later then?

LINDA: Listen Birdman, you're doing my head in. I said no.
   N.O. You're making the place look untidy. Go play with
   your friends.

   Pause.

BIRDMAN: You okay Linda?

LINDA: I will be when you go.

BIRDMAN: What you do to your arm?

LINDA: What? Knocked it.

BIRDMAN: It's burnt.

LINDA: Yeah. I burnt it.

BIRDMAN: Your mum in?

LINDA: No. She's at work. But that doesn't mean you can stay. In fact it means you've got to go. Bye Birdman.

BIRDMAN: Linda.

LINDA: Bye Birdman.

> Holding open the door.
> Noon sun pouring in.
> He's got freckles.
> Birdman.
> Birdboy.
> Touch his arm as he passes.
> Yeah go on Birdman. You stick him for me.
> Make his six-pack grin.

Scene Three

BIRDMAN's foster home.
The SOCIAL WORKER, sorting out her papers in a briefcase.

SOCIAL WORKER: Birdman. Not really my call. Two-ish. I can't be more exact than that. I've lost my watch. But it would be about two-ish, because I noticed the time on the clock as I paid at the toll-bridge. I love the drive across that bridge. For five minutes you swoop across the river, lifted up above the water, looking down on all the little doll's houses and the little doll-people, and the children playing on the boats. Some daredevil hanging onto the high-point about to dive in. Don't fancy his chances. But I don't get out.

As I said – I've lost my watch. Or maybe that's the kind way to put it. Actually they knicked it. Someone did. One of them. It was a long time ago. I never replaced it. I just got used to guessing the time, and being late for appointments is part of the job. They don't like you for it. But they don't like me anyway.

(*Pause.*)

They've got other things to do.

(*Pause.*)

And I'm usually a disappointment.

(*Pause.*)

There's nothing I can do to hide these rings of sweat I get. I know it makes them dislike me. Jesus Christ. It's not my fault. And my feet hurt. Jesus Christ. I don't know why it happens.

Don't ask me why it happens.

What do I know? Some careless god flicked a pebble up in space and it landed here. Jesus Christ.

Open the door and let's get going.

Smiling now –

Birdman at the door

Ah! Birdman!

BIRDMAN: Don't call me that.

You got no right to call me that.

SOCIAL WORKER: Fine. (*Consulting her papers.*) I thought Karen – your regular social worker is Karen isn't it?

Pause. BIRDMAN doesn't reply.

Well I thought she left a note saying that was what you liked to be called.

BIRDMAN: To you it's Joey.

SOCIAL WORKER: Fine. My mistake then. I'll get Karen to take that note out.
(*Pause.*)
(*Smiling.*) Joey.
How's things?
Cool trainers.
Good haircut.

BIRDMAN: You always say that.

SOCIAL WORKER: I don't believe we've met before.

BIRDMAN: You're all the same. You all say the same thing.

SOCIAL WORKER: Fine. Well. My name's Jan, by the way.
(*Pause.*)
How's things?

BIRDMAN: You already said that.

SOCIAL WORKER: Just testing you.

BIRDMAN: Yeah, right.

SOCIAL WORKER: Well. Joey. Shall we have a cup of tea?

BIRDMAN: No. Just get down to it.

SOCIAL WORKER: Right. Well. You talked to your social worker about a new placement. Because this one isn't suitable. Right?
(*Beat.*)
Well. We've been looking for a new placement.

BIRDMAN: And?

SOCIAL WORKER: And it's good news and bad news. It's a bit of both.

BIRDMAN: Meaning?

SOCIAL WORKER: Well. I've found you a new placement.
(*Pause.*)
It's a family with teenagers. They're used to taking teenagers. That's good isn't it?

Pause.

BIRDMAN: So what's bad about it?

SOCIAL WORKER: It's quite a way from here. Well. Not to beat about the bush – It's in Birmingham.

BIRDMAN: Birmingham! But that's up north. It's miles away. I'm not going.

SOCIAL WORKER: Joey. We've talked about this – your social worker talked to you about this. You can't stay here. This isn't an appropriate placement. You need to go somewhere more suitable for you. Somewhere you can stay for longer.

BIRDMAN: I'm not going.

SOCIAL WORKER: You should at least visit.

BIRDMAN: I'm not going.

SOCIAL WORKER: I hear you're uncomfortable at the thought of going.

BIRDMAN: I'm not going.

SOCIAL WORKER: I hear you're uncomfortable at the thought of going. So I'll leave you to get used to the idea. Sue needs the space for her own family. She's not kitted out for long term placements with teenagers. We always knew this was only a temporary placement didn't we? I'm sure Karen never disguised that fact.
(*Pause.*)

We need to move you in two weeks. Sue will help you
pack your things.
(*Beat.*)
It's for the best Joey.
(*Beat.*)
Isn't it hot?

BIRDMAN: I'm not going.

SOCIAL WORKER: Goodbye Joey. I expect Karen will be
back off leave soon, and you can talk to her. She'll be
able to tell you all about it.

BIRDMAN: I'm not going.

SOCIAL WORKER: I'll see myself out. Goodness it's hot.
Goodbye.

Scene Four

Riverbank.
SITA, MEL, MARIE.

SITA: After three, before four.
Easy, yeah –
we're on our way to the park
on the path along the river.
Mel – hobbling –
'cos she's wearing stupid shoes,
so we can't go that fast.
Taking forever.
Marie, moaning 'cos it's hot.
Why's she wearing that jacket?
Just because her aunt said
it took pounds off her.
We met at ten.
Haven't had lunch.

Tide's out –
Stinking river.
That's where Marie went in one night.
Riding on a trolley.
Broke her arm.
We laughed.
Marie howling in the mud.
We had to go and get her.
After three, before four
Birdman's coming down river.

Birdman!
Birdman going on past.

MEL: Hey, Birdman, she's talking to you.

MARIE: Yeah, she's talking to you. You trying to be rude or
something?

BIRDMAN: No. What?

MARIE: Where you going Birdbrain?

BIRDMAN: Birmingham.

SITA: What, now? You got no suitcase. Where's your gear?

MEL: She means *now*, where you going *now*?

BIRDMAN: Dunno really. Just walking. I suppose.

MARIE: Well keep walking then. Ta ta.

SITA: We're going up the park.

MEL: Sita! We don't want him tagging along.

MARIE: No. Doh-brain. No taggers-on. Specially not little boys.

SITA's phone rings. It's a text message.

MEL: Who's that then?

SITA: It's my mum. She wants to know where I am. She always wants to know where I am.

MEL: Tell her we're round my house.

SITA: Too close.

MARIE: Tell her you're round Linda's.

MEL: Yeah. Tell her you're round Linda's. She's not allowed out.

MARIE: She's grounded.

BIRDMAN: Why?

Silence.

MEL: None of yours.

BIRDMAN: Why?

MARIE: What's it to you? You fancy her?

MEL: What, Linda? You fancy Linda?

BIRDMAN: Why's she grounded?

MARIE: Girls' stuff. Little boy. Now run along. We've got things to do. Places to go. People to see. Know what I mean?

MEL: Bye Birdman.

SITA: Birdman, bye. See you later down the park?

MARIE: Not if we can help it.

Scene Five

The park along the riverbank.
NIALL and TOM are lying in the grass.

NIALL: Park.
Just hanging.
Too hot. Shade's moved. We haven't.
Pegged out in the sun.
There's a buzzing noise coming in at us from across the water.
Gobs of sound going drip, drip in the middle of my forehead.
My stomach's curling in this heat.

Pause.

TOM: Niall?
Niall?

NIALL: What is it?

TOM: What time?

NIALL: Is it?

TOM: Yeah. What time is it?

NIALL: Dunno.
(*Pause.*)
It was two.

TOM: That was hours ago. It must be at least four.

NIALL: At the clock, it was two.

TOM: You've been asleep.

NIALL: Have not. Maybe.

TOM: Get some chips?

NIALL: You got any money?

TOM: No. You?

NIALL: No.

TOM: I think I might go home.

NIALL: What for?

TOM: Food. I'm hungry.

NIALL: Bring us something.

TOM: Don't your mum feed you?

NIALL: Not if she can help it.

TOM: She's dead tight your mum.

NIALL: It's not her. It's her boyfriend. She's all right. He thinks if they don't feed us, we'll go and live somewhere else.

TOM: He's dead tight.

NIALL: He's not going to last.

TOM: They never do with your mum.

NIALL: It's not her fault. She's all right. She just can't tell a good bloke from a bad one.

TOM: Maybe she should give it a rest.

NIALL: Maybe. You going to get us some food then?

TOM: In a minute.

NIALL's phone rings. It's a text message

Who's that from?

Pause as he reads.

NIALL: I wish she wouldn't do that.

TOM: Who is it? Marie?

NIALL: Marie? No way. It's Kirsty. She always puts loads of kisses. I wish she wouldn't do that.

TOM: You don't do it back?

NIALL: Nah. Well, some. I kind of think – she expects it.

TOM: Well weak.

NIALL: That's just girls isn't it? What they expect?

TOM: You meeting her tonight?

NIALL: She's not allowed out down the park.

TOM: She's not allowed out with you, you mean.

NIALL: Maybe.
Have you met her mum?

TOM: No. You?

NIALL jumps up and waves.

NIALL: She wouldn't speak to me.

She wouldn't speak to me. Standing in her doorway, holding onto that brass knocker, puffing out her chest. I saw it. That look. I know it. That look. It just says – dirt. You're a piece of dirt. That's what it says. Looks at my feet. That's enough. I know that look. Breathes deep. Stitches her lips together. Breathes deep and turns away. Walks deep into the house, calling Kirsty. Hissing Ki-irssty. Jabber jabber jabber. Course she's not coming out. Not with me at any rate.

Hey! Birdman! Birdman!

BIRDMAN turns.

TOM: What did you call him over for?

NIALL: Hey Birdman. Az is looking for you.

BIRDMAN: So?

NIALL: Just telling you. That's all. You fishing tonight?
(*Pause.*)
Meet you up Stonebridge later?

Pause. BIRDMAN stands and looks.

TOM: His brains is fried.

NIALL: We'll be there about eight. Got stuff to do before then.
(*Pause.*)
See you then.

BIRDMAN: Is Linda going?

TOM: (*Laughing.*) It's too late for her.

BIRDMAN: What? What did he mean by that?

NIALL: She's not allowed out is she?

BIRDMAN: I heard that. What does he mean it's too late?

TOM: Too many questions Birdman. Too hot to talk.
(*Pause.*)
Do you fancy her? Do you? Loser you.

NIALL: I'm starving. Come on Tom. Let's go and get some food.

They move off and leave BIRDMAN, who seems undecided about what to do next.

Scene Six

SAL is hiding in the shadows. She comes out and speaks as BIRDMAN lingers. He kicks some rubbish around for a while, then leaves.

SAL: I see them. I see them all from my hidey-hole. They don't see me. Watching them. I've got my eye on them all. And Birdman. Especially Birdman. What's up with him? There's something up with him. I know.

The SOCIAL WORKER comes on. Takes a plastic bag out of her briefcase, spreads it on the ground, sits on it, takes off her shoes. Begins to smoke.

You'll get muck on your skirt.

SOCIAL WORKER: I'm sorry?

SAL: There's a bench down there. You don't have to sit in the dirt.

SOCIAL WORKER: That's all right. I'm prepared. (*She indicates the plastic bag.*) Am I in your space?

SAL: No.

SOCIAL WORKER: You don't sound too sure about that. I won't be long. Just stopping for a breather.

SAL: You shouldn't smoke. Then you won't get out of breath.

SOCIAL WORKER: True. Really I just stopped because it's hot. It just takes it out of me, this heat.

SAL: You a teacher?

SOCIAL WORKER: No.
What makes you say that?

SAL: My teacher has shoes like that.

SOCIAL WORKER: They don't fit me. They hurt my feet. Maybe I should get some different shoes.

SAL: So you won't look like a teacher?

SOCIAL WORKER: Just so I can walk without limping, actually. It would help.

SAL: I'm sure you could still be a teacher, if you like.

SOCIAL WORKER: What, even with the wrong shoes? Thanks, but I don't like.

SAL: What are you then?

SOCIAL WORKER: What am I?

SAL: So what do you do?

SOCIAL WORKER: That's a good question. Actually. I've been trying to answer that myself this morning. What do I do?
I take a piece of paper. I go to see someone or they come to see me.
I talk they don't listen. I listen, they don't talk.
Then they ask me questions I can't answer. Then I put the piece of paper back in the file it came from.

SAL: You are a teacher.

SOCIAL WORKER: Do you like your teacher?

SAL: Not really.
You shouldn't smoke.

SOCIAL WORKER: I know.

SAL: Mr Hill smokes in the art cupboard.

SOCIAL WORKER: I like the sound of Mr Hill.
What about you? Are you here all by yourself?

SAL: My brother's around.

SOCIAL WORKER: Does he know where you are?

SAL: Why?

SOCIAL WORKER: This is a lonely part of the park.

SAL: I'm not lonely. I've got a den.

SOCIAL WORKER: Well that's all right then. You've got
somewhere to go.
I have to go now. Got another appointment.

SAL: You could stay a bit longer. If you wanted.

SOCIAL WORKER: Thanks. I'm late already. It's all too late.
But it won't wait.

SAL: You've left your plastic bag.

Scene Seven

LINDA's house.

AARON: My turn now.

LINDA: No. No. It's me.

AARON: What you?

LINDA: Yes. Me.
Birdman comes round my house.
Knocks on my door.

MEL: What again? What does he want from you?

LINDA: I don't know do I?
Asking things I haven't got the words to answer.

See this.
There's a knock at my door.
I can see it's him.
But I'm not opening up.

BIRDMAN one side of the door, LINDA the other.

BIRDMAN: Linda. Linda.

LINDA: What? What you want Birdman?
I told you to go away this morning.
What you want?

BIRDMAN: Talk to you.

LINDA: Yeah.

BIRDMAN: Really.

LINDA: What about?

BIRDMAN: What happened.
What happened Linda?

LINDA: I don't know what you're talking about.

BIRDMAN: You do. What happened?

LINDA: None of yours. If you're here, you know what
happened.

BIRDMAN: Open up Linda. Let me in.

LINDA: Go away Birdman.

BIRDMAN: Just for a moment. Please Linda.

LINDA: No.

BIRDMAN: Please. It's really important.

LINDA: I'm going upstairs now. You can shout all you like.
I'm not going to let you in.

(*She moves away.*)
I'm not listening Birdman.

*LINDA moves off and hides her head, so she can't hear
BIRDMAN shouting.*

BIRDMAN: Linda! Linda!

BIRDMAN turns on his heel and walks off.

Scene Eight

AARON with two rods.

AARON: Now it's me.
Sun still glancing from the west off the river.
So it's seven-ish. Way after six.
Nettle, thistle, bramble, dock
choke that path around the manor.
Further up the water's slimmer,
faster, sliding through the park.
I'm heading up to Stonebridge,
it squats in the river. Sits beyond the tide-head.
It's where the fishing's better.

Round the bend – see Birdman chucking stones in the
water.

*BIRDMAN is sitting, gazing out across the water.
Occasionally flipping stones.*

All still.

Hey Birdman.

BIRDMAN grunts.

Not talking then.

Birdman, hey.

Girl.

BIRDMAN: What. What is it. What do you want?

AARON: Going fishing. Stonebridge. You coming?

BIRDMAN: Why would I want to do that?

AARON: You might catch something. I've got a spare rod.
(*Pause.*)
You waiting for someone?
(*Pause.*)
I said you waiting for someone?

BIRDMAN: No.

AARON: You coming then?

BIRDMAN gets up.

So that's how we get there.
Me in front, Birdman behind. Silent.
Sal behind him –
I know she's there, even though she pretends not to be.
I've seen her.

SITA, MEL, MARIE, TOM, NIALL are on the bank of the river.

TOM: Hey Aaron. Lend us that rod.

AARON: It's for Birdman.

He gives BIRDMAN the rod. BIRDMAN gives it to TOM.

Why did you do that?

BIRDMAN: Don't need it. Don't want it.

AARON: I thought we wanted to fish today?

BIRDMAN: You wanted to.

AARON: Yeah. Right. What you using for bait Tom?

TOM: (*Shrugs.*) Bread? You got maggots?

AARON: Don't need maggots.

TOM casts his line.

You're casting in the wrong place doh-nut. You're casting where the current runs, you've got to stay along the bank.

AARON threads his line. TOM and AARON fish. The girls sit on the bank with NIALL. BIRDMAN sits to one side.

MEL: *Ich angele gern.*

MARIE: What?

MEL: *Ich angele gern.*

SITA: I like fishing.

MEL: *Fantastisch.*

MARIE: Whatever.
(*Pause.*)
I'm never going to speak another word of German again.

MEL: You never spoke a word of German before.

MARIE: Well. I'm never going to walk in that classroom again. And that woman's never going to ask me to speak another word of German.
(*Pause.*)
Hey Birdman – they speak German in Birmingham don't they?

BIRDMAN: Shut it Marie.

MARIE: Ooh. Now that's not very nice is it? Did you hear that Sita? That wasn't very nice was it? You packed your case yet Birdman? Don't hang about on our account.

BIRDMAN moves further away.

Oh I thought you was going then Birdman. I was just getting ready for an emotional goodbye scene. Where's my tissue? Anybody got a tissue?

SITA: Leave it out Marie.

MARIE: I will when I want to. Not because you say.

MEL: Niall's good at German, aren't you Niall?

MARIE: He's not.

MEL: He is. He got the top mark for a boy.

MARIE: She just likes him, that's all. She likes all the boys.

MEL: Niall's only got to open his mouth and he's *fantastisch.*

MARIE: He's what?

SITA: Fantastic.

MARIE: Yeah well. She's a lesbian isn't she.

SITA: So she likes boys?

MARIE: Covering her tracks.

SITA: Oh.

AARON has caught something – he's pulling on the line.

MEL: Aaron's caught something. Az's got a bite. Hold on Az. Hold on.

They all jump up and run to the water's edge, commenting, encouraging AARON as he fights with the line – eventually he lands a fish. They all crowd round and look.

SITA: What's he going to do now? He's got to get it off the hook. Oh I can't look.

NIALL: Oh you beauty. It's huge Az.

TOM: What is it?

AARON: Carp, I think. Not sure, really.
(*He unhooks the fish.*)
Where's the bucket?

TOM: Here.

NIALL: It needs water in it, doh-brain.

TOM: (*Scoops water into the bucket.*) Here.

MEL: It's too big for the bucket Az. Its head's gonna stick out.

MARIE: Oh my God. See it wriggle. It makes me feel sick. Put it back.

SITA: Yeah Aaron. Put it back. Look at its eyes.

AARON: Stick its head in. It's got to breathe.

SITA: What you going to do with it? You're not going to eat it are you?

SAL comes out from the shadows.

SAL: Don't kill it yet. I'm going to get mum. She's got to see this. She'll never believe you if she doesn't see it.

AARON: No don't do that.

SAL: Why not? She'll want to see it. I'll tell her to bring the camera. She can take a photo.

AARON: Don't do that. Don't bring her here.

SAL: I'm going anyway.

AARON: You stay here Sal. You're not going anywhere.

SAL: You can't stop me.

Exit SAL.

MEL: Can I hold it Az?

SITA: Oh no Mel. Don't do that. It's disgusting.

MARIE: Go on then Sita. You hold it. Go on. Touch it.

SITA: No. I can't. I'll be sick.

MARIE: Go on Sita. Touch it. Touch it I said. Go on. (*Pause.*)
You scared?

*SITA hesitates a moment, but MARIE is looking at her hard.
She touches the fish.*

Yeuch. Smelly. Don't come near me with your smelly
fingers.

SITA: Well you didn't touch it did you? You wouldn't do it.

MARIE: I will. Watch this. Give it here.

*She takes the fish. The others jeer. Then they pass the fish
round. NIALL drops it. TOM stamps on it, then kicks it in
the river.*

AARON: While we're passing round the fish, Birdman goes.
Doesn't say anything. Doesn't say where he's going. Just
takes off. I didn't notice he'd gone until later.

Scene Nine

RACHEL's house.

RACHEL: It was after eight when I saw Birdman.
How I know –

it's a bit complicated – I'll start at the beginning.
Me sitting listening for Col –
he's always late –
sitting listening to that little gold clock on the
mantelshelf.
It chimes on the half-hour – just once
then on the full hour it does the whole works –
me sitting listening to it chime eight times –
he's late he's late he's late he's late.
Me sitting listening on the edge of my seat –
I can't sit back because I'll put creases in my top.
At eight he's late.
Well late.

I'm beginning to think he's gone off with someone else
Mel or Linda or Jackie or Marie – they'd all go with
him –
he's only got to whistle.
That's a line from a film, but he meant it nice.
I mean – they're dogs – and they're nothing to him.
I'm beginning to think I'll chuck that little gold clock
out the window
I'm beginning to think I'm not feeling too good – I'm
beginning to shrink on the inside, and my mouth's all dry.
Then the doorbell rings.

Doorbell.

That's him.
And in a minute we're gonna go out
and in a minute we're gonna kiss
and in a minute we're gonna get all loved-up.

Hang on a minute Col. I just need to get my shoes.
Where's my handbag? Okay.

Outside – at the car.

COLIN: Da-da!

RACHEL: Where's the van?

COLIN: My dad's got it.

RACHEL: Is this his car then?

COLIN: Yeah.

RACHEL: Borrowed it?

COLIN: Yeah.

RACHEL: Does he know?

COLIN: Course not.

RACHEL: Well we can't go out in it then.

COLIN: It doesn't matter.

RACHEL: It does.

COLIN: It doesn't. Because he thinks Phil's got it.

RACHEL: Oh.

COLIN: All right now?

RACHEL: Yeah. I guess. Where's Phil then?

COLIN: Dropped him off round Gary's house. They've got business.

RACHEL: What kind of business does your brother do?

Pause.

COLIN: Look, are you coming or not? I can always get someone else, if you don't want to come.

RACHEL: I'm coming.

COLIN: Get in then.

They get in the car.

RACHEL: It's nice.

COLIN: Yeah.

RACHEL: It's really nice. Nice colour.

COLIN: Persian silver.

RACHEL: Does the CD work?

COLIN: Course it does.

RACHEL: Really nice. Where are we going then?

COLIN: Up Spike Hill.

RACHEL: Not the pub?

COLIN: We'll do Spike Hill then the pub.

RACHEL: How fast does it go?

COLIN: Faster than you'd want to know.

RACHEL: Go on then. Show me.

COLIN: Just shout if it gets too fast. Shall we have the roof down?

RACHEL: Yeah.

COLIN: That fast enough?

RACHEL: It doesn't go any faster, does it?

COLIN: Course it does.

RACHEL: Slow down now Col. We're coming up to Millers Bend. Colin. Slow down. What are you doing? Put your hands on the wheel Colin. I said on the wheel.

COLIN: You scared Rachel?

RACHEL: Course I'm bloody scared. You're going too fast.

COLIN: Ah. Chicken.

RACHEL: Stop the car. Stop the car Colin. Let me out.

COLIN: All right. All right. I'll slow down. I'm slowing down now, see?

RACHEL: Slower. Go slower.

COLIN: Like this?

RACHEL: Both hands. Drive with both hands. And both feet.

COLIN: Like this?

RACHEL: Both feet at once, both hands at once.

COLIN: Like this?

RACHEL: Don't look at me, look at the road.
Okay. Stop the car. Stop the car now.

She gets out.

COLIN: Where are you going? It's miles to the pub.

RACHEL: I'll walk.

He's driving along beside her.

COLIN: Get back in the car Rachel. Come on, get back in the car.

RACHEL: No.

COLIN: Last chance?

RACHEL: No.

So he goes off, burning rubber.
I'm in a huff –
these shoes aren't meant for walking

and my top's all creased.
Then I hear it –
it's somebody screaming.
Sounds like murder
and she won't last much longer.

She stops. Listens all about her. She is rooted to the spot.
BIRDMAN comes.

(*Whispers.*) Birdman. Birdman.

BIRDMAN: Fox. It's a fox. Calling for its mate.

RACHEL: Oh. Oh. I thought.
(*She laughs.*)
I thought it was.

BIRDMAN: It's a fox.

Pause.

RACHEL: What you doing round here?

BIRDMAN: Been to see my sister.

RACHEL: Natalie? I thought she moved away.

BIRDMAN: Not Natalie. Gloria – she's my big sister.

RACHEL: I didn't know you had a big sister.

Pause.

BIRDMAN: She wasn't in.
Walking home now. You?

RACHEL: I was out with Colin.
(*Pause.*)
He's gone now.

BIRDMAN: You walking then?

RACHEL: I guess.

BIRDMAN: Why do you go with him?

RACHEL: What? Why do you want to know?

BIRDMAN: Why?

RACHEL: You wouldn't understand.

BIRDMAN: When you know you're not the only one?
You do know you're not the only one, don't you?

RACHEL: I know.
But – it doesn't stop him kissing me the way he kisses me.
It doesn't stop me from liking it.
(*Pause.*)
Besides. It's none of yours. You ask too many questions.

BIRDMAN: Cut through the track to the park?

RACHEL: I don't really like it. It'll be dark soon.

BIRDMAN: Go on. It'll save us ten minutes. I'll hold your
hand if you're scared.

RACHEL: Shove off. I'm not scared.

BIRDMAN: Come on then.

RACHEL: So we cut through the track.
I really don't like it.
It's full of nettles. And old mattresses. A fridge.
Things that don't rot.
You could fill a house with all this junk.
Then.
We see her.
She's lying in the last patch of sun.

BIRDMAN: Vixen.

RACHEL: I swear to you she sees us.
She turns and looks right at us.
But it doesn't make her move.
She's not moving.
She's not a scabby fox at all.
She's rich and glossy.
I'm thinking it's like one of those books you read at the dentists.
I'm thinking it's almost a good thing I got out of the car.
I'm thinking it's a good thing we came down the track.

BIRDMAN grabs RACHEL and tries to kiss her. RACHEL struggles and pulls away. She looks at him.

Get off Birdman, what do you think you're doing? Get your paws off me.

Birdman says nothing.
Just turns and walks off quickly.
I have to follow him. Not staying here on my own.
Then at the road, he disappears.

Scene Ten

At the Stonebridge – dusk.

AARON: It's not dark yet. But it's getting there. Things are coming to a head.

SITA: I don't see that. I didn't see that.

TOM: I didn't see it coming, did you?

AARON: We're all gathered at the water. Standing in the grey light at the water's edge. Same as yesterday and the day before.
We're all tied to this ribbon of dirty water.

SITA: Aaron's mum didn't come. It's better that way.

TOM: We chucked that fish back in.
  It floated a bit.

MEL: Drifted downstream. Then disappeared.

AARON: What would she have done? Nothing much.

SAL: Taken a photo. She could have brought the camera
  and taken a photo. For the family album.

AARON: In your dreams Sal. But you don't give up, do you?

SITA: But there's still that boy.
  Tell the story of that boy.

SAL: Why do you call him that? He's still got a name.

NIALL: But later on,
  After it's all drifted down the river
  He'll be just another boy who…

SAL: What do you mean?

NIALL: You know what I mean.
  People will say, 'There was that boy…'

MARIE: 'What boy'

NIALL: 'That boy from round here who…'

SAL: Birdman. You mean Birdman.

MEL: For the moment, yeah…

SITA: Then tell the story.

SAL: No. You. I don't like the next bit.

TOM: What's to like or dislike about it?
  It's just a story about a boy from round here who
  kept coming back to the river.

NIALL: What? No that's not it. He asked too many questions.

TOM: What? No. Did he?

NIALL: I said: he kept asking questions.

AARON: It's true. He's right.
   He kept asking questions.

SITA: So there was this boy who kept asking questions.

MEL: Then what happened?

SAL: I don't like this bit.

AARON: Shut up and tell it. Just tell it.

*Everyone is standing and sitting around on the bank of the
river, some with cans they share around.
Music is coming from the car. AARON and NIALL are fishing.
TOM and COLIN are sitting with MEL and SITA and MARIE.
SAL sits a little apart.*

BIRDMAN arrives.

SAL: Birdman.

BIRDMAN: You should be at home.

SAL: Says who?

BIRDMAN: Go home.

SAL: Why?

BIRDMAN: It's too late for you.

SAL: Mum's not in.

BIRDMAN: (*To AARON.*) Take her home.

AARON: I'm fishing.

BIRDMAN: She shouldn't be here. What's she drinking?
What's that you're drinking Sal?

AARON: What's the matter with you? She likes it here. And
I'm fishing.

BIRDMAN: What's she doing here?

AARON: She's not doing anything. Now shut up. I'm fishing.

RACHEL arrives. COLIN sees her. She sees him.

MEL: Rachel. Hi.
Nice top.

RACHEL: Thanks.

MEL: Looks special.

RACHEL: It's new yeah.

SITA: Az caught a fish. It was gross.

RACHEL: Where is it?

SITA: Swam off. No it didn't. Kind of floated off, then sank.
I think. It was kind of sad, wasn't it Marie?

MARIE: No. Not half as sad as that cat we found.

MEL: Yeah. That was sad. It still had its bell. It almost lived.

TOM: I tell you cats can't swim. I guarantee.
You wouldn't believe me.

MARIE: That was sad. It tried though, didn't it? You
shouldn't have thrown it in.

TOM: You should have believed me.

SITA: Someone might have missed that cat. Wondered what
happened to it.

Perhaps they put food out, and then they went to call it.
And it never came back.

MEL: It was funny though, the way it skated in the air.

MARIE: Yeah. That was funny.

RACHEL takes off her shoes, dangles her feet in the water.

MEL: What you doing Rachel? The fish'll get your toes.
That one Az caught had teeth.

RACHEL: My feet hurt.

MARIE: You walked from home?

RACHEL: Might have.

MARIE: You walking home after?

RACHEL: Might be.

Pause.

MARIE: Hey Col. You taking us all home later?

COLIN: No room tonight.

COLIN gets up.

MARIE: Where you going Col?

COLIN: None of yours.

*COLIN walks off to go and sit in the car. RACHEL gets up
and goes to join him.*

RACHEL: You got room for me later?

COLIN: Dunno. Got some things to do.

RACHEL: What things?

COLIN: Just things.
You took your time getting here.

RACHEL: It's a long way from Millers Bend.

COLIN: You didn't have to get out.

RACHEL: I was scared.

COLIN: You didn't have to get out.

RACHEL: Col.

She puts her hand on his arm.

COLIN: What?

COLIN clucks quietly, like a chicken. RACHEL turns and walks off. Puts on her shoes.

Where are you going?

RACHEL: Home.

COLIN: Don't expect a lift.

RACHEL: Don't want one.

COLIN: Hey Mel, Marie – do you want a lift?

MEL: We're walking.

COLIN: Sita – I'm going round Linda's do you want a lift?

SITA: I'm walking.

BIRDMAN looks up.

RACHEL: Shove off Colin.

COLIN laughs. Then goes over to NIALL and TOM.

COLIN: Hey Rachel, come here. Come on. Come over here.

RACHEL: I'm going home.

COLIN: It was only a joke Rachel. Come back.

He goes and puts his arm around RACHEL. She shakes him off, he grabs her again. She winds out of his embrace.

Come on.

BIRDMAN: Leave her alone.

COLIN: What?

BIRDMAN: Leave her alone.

COLIN: Stop twittering Birdman.

BIRDMAN faces up to COLIN.

RACHEL: Keep out of this Birdman.

BIRDMAN: Why do you do that? Why are you sticking up for him?

RACHEL: What is it to you?

BIRDMAN: Why do you let him do that to you?

COLIN: Hang on a minute. What's going on? What is she to you?

RACHEL: Nothing. It's nothing Col. Shut up Birdman. Just keep out of this.

BIRDMAN: No I won't. I won't shut up.
Why don't you ask him what happened to Linda?
Go on. Ask him.
You won't will you? You afraid of what he'll say?
Or maybe you know. You know, but you don't want to know.
If it's not him it's someone else.
Don't you ever ask your friends what happens to them at night?
You never ask do you?
You just don't want to know do you?

Don't you ever wonder about it? Why it's them and not
you. What they've done to deserve it.
Why it's them and not someone else?
Why don't you ever ask why it happens?

BIRDMAN runs and gets in the car. Locks the door. COLIN
runs and bangs on the outside. Shouting at BIRDMAN.

COLIN: Get out the car Birdman. You bloody madman. Get
out. I'll tear your head off. Get out.

COLIN carries on shouting. The others watch from a distance.
BIRDMAN turns up the music.
BIRDMAN stares straight ahead, drives off – COLIN is flung
back.

Scene Eleven

LINDA in the house.

LINDA: I hear him.
I hear him moving around outside the house.
Round the doors, round the windows.
Trying to get in.

I can hear you, Birdman.
What you want now?

BIRDMAN: I just want to hang around with you for a while.

LINDA: Who sent you?

BIRDMAN: No one.

LINDA: What you want?

BIRDMAN: I'm just here to hang around, okay?

LINDA: Hang around. Hang around. What does that mean?

BIRDMAN: I'll just be here while the clock ticks, okay?
It's just the clock ticking, and I'm here.

LINDA: I can't let you in the house.

BIRDMAN: Then I'll hang around outside. I'll sit here, so
you know where I am. You can be inside where the
clock ticks, and I'll sit here.

BIRDMAN sits down. LINDA is on the inside, listening.

LINDA: Listen Birdman, I can hear the clock tick but I can't
hear you.
Can't you breathe more loudly or something? (*Pause.*)
Birdman? You still there?

BIRDMAN: I'm still here. How much time has gone?

LINDA: I don't know. I didn't look at the clock, did I?

BIRDMAN: I think it goes slowly. Time passes slowly when
you're hanging around.

LINDA: Yeah well. When you're having fun. It's a daft idea
anyway.
Passing the time like this. It's a stupid idea.

BIRDMAN: Then let me in.

LINDA: I already told you, I can't do that.

BIRDMAN: Well come outside. Come on. Come outside and
sit in the car.

LINDA: You got a car?

BIRDMAN: Yeah. Come for a spin.

LINDA: We're just passing time in the car?

BIRDMAN: Yeah.

LINDA: Till when?

BIRDMAN: Whenever you like.

LINDA: Then you'll take me home?

BIRDMAN: Wherever you like.

LINDA comes out of the house, smiles when she sees the car.
BIRDMAN holds open the door for her. She gets in.

LINDA: No questions.

BIRDMAN: No questions.

LINDA: No touching.

BIRDMAN: None of that.

LINDA: Where shall we go?

BIRDMAN: You want to see some foxes?

Scene Twelve

At the track.
BIRDMAN and LINDA get out of the car. LINDA stumbles.

LINDA: Ouch. I've ricked my ankle. I can't see a thing.
Shine the torch this way a bit more.

They pick their way across the track, move amongst the
rubbish.

You're sure there are foxes here?

BIRDMAN: Yeah. I saw the vixen earlier on. Look, sit up here.

LINDA: What about you?

BIRDMAN: I'll sit over here.

LINDA: Give me the torch though.

BIRDMAN: All right. You can have the torch.

LINDA sits on top of the fridge, takes the torch. She shines it on BIRDMAN.

BIRDMAN: What you doing that for?

LINDA: Just looking.

BIRDMAN: Just don't shine it in my eyes, that's all.

She shines it in his eyes, moves it over his face, shines it in his eyes again. He puts his hands over his face. They wait. LINDA tires after a while, and gets down and begins to look through the rubbish. She opens the fridge door, shuts it again. Moves on.

LINDA: Birdman.

BIRDMAN: That's me.

LINDA: What's your real name?

BIRDMAN: No questions. We said no questions. We're just passing the time.

LINDA: Hm. Birdman.

BIRDMAN: Yeah. Is it a question?

LINDA: Kind of. Not about you though. Can I ask it?

BIRDMAN: You can ask it. What if I don't know the answer?

LINDA: You make it up.

BIRDMAN: And then you guess if it's right?

LINDA: Could do. Yeah.

BIRDMAN: Okay then.

LINDA: Birdman. How many bones in a body?

BIRDMAN: What?

LINDA: If you break all the bones in your body, how many do you break?

BIRDMAN: I dunno. Fifty? A hundred? Do you think that's right?

LINDA: More I reckon. Must be more. If you look at your fingers, think about your toes. And there must be loads of other ones all over the place. If you think about it. You're wrong I reckon.

BIRDMAN: I don't get the prize then.

LINDA: You don't get the prize. Have another go?

BIRDMAN: Not so hard this time.

LINDA: Just keep your eye on the prize Birdman.

BIRDMAN: I keep my eye on the prize. What is the prize?

LINDA: You find out when you win. You have to win first.

BIRDMAN: What's the question then?

LINDA sits back up on the fridge, thinks for a minute.

LINDA: How long can a human being be without air?

BIRDMAN: Linda. Can't you ask a proper question?

LINDA: It is a proper question.

BIRDMAN: A different question then.

LINDA: How long before you faint if you don't get any air?

BIRDMAN: Hell I don't know. Two minutes?

LINDA: Two minutes.

BIRDMAN: You think I'm right?

LINDA: I think you're right.

BIRDMAN: Yes!! So I get the prize! And the prize is?

LINDA picks up an old crash-helmet from the fridge and gives it to BIRDMAN.

LINDA: Here, the champion's crown.

BIRDMAN: Really? I really get to wear the champion's crown? Great. Fantastic.

He puts it on. LINDA slides off the fridge and stands beside it.

LINDA: Now shut me in.

BIRDMAN: What?

LINDA: You shut me in.

BIRDMAN: No.

LINDA: Shut me in Birdman.

BIRDMAN: No. I won't do it.

LINDA: You can let me out again.

BIRDMAN: How long?

LINDA: Two minutes.

BIRDMAN: That's too long.

LINDA: Just hang around. You do two minutes there. I'm two minutes here.

LINDA gets in the fridge.

BIRDMAN: It's dangerous.

LINDA: Two minutes. It's not. That's a fact. There's air in there.

BIRDMAN: Why?

LINDA: I just need you to shut me up. That's all.

BIRDMAN: Only two minutes then. That's all. No more.
  After two minutes I'm opening up.

LINDA: Not before. Have you got a watch?

BIRDMAN: No.

LINDA: You can have mine. It's got a second hand here. Look.

BIRDMAN: I don't want to do this.

LINDA: Close the door Birdman.

*BIRDMAN takes the torch and closes the door to the fridge.
He stands beside it. Walks away from it. Comes back
and puts his arms around it. For two minutes he hugs the
fridge, tapping his fingers gently on the outside.*

BIRDMAN: Linda. Linda.

*He checks the watch, at two minutes he tears open the
fridge door, and LINDA falls out. BIRDMAN grabs her. Then
she opens her eyes and laughs. She gets up quickly,*

LINDA: I said no touching, Birdman.

BIRDMAN: Sod you, Linda. Don't do that again.

LINDA smiles.

LINDA: We could stay here. Got a fridge. Got some chairs.

BIRDMAN: We could live here.

LINDA: We could make a roof.

BIRDMAN: We don't need a roof.

LINDA: We will need a roof when it rains. I'm not getting
  wet. I haven't got my big coat.

BIRDMAN starts to pull bits of junk into place to create a makeshift roof.

BIRDMAN: That's our roof.

LINDA brings over a mattress and/or some rags.

LINDA: That's my bed. Where are you going to sleep? You can sleep on a chair. Two chairs.

BIRDMAN: I'm on guard. I'll sleep outside, look at the stars.

LINDA: Well if it rains, you can come in. That'll be your space there. You'll always sit there. And sometimes I'll come out and look at the stars.

LINDA sits down on a chair, looking out.

What you going to do with that car Birdman? It can't stay there.
It's all over the garden. It's spoiling the view.

BIRDMAN: Dunno. Take it back I suppose. Better do it tonight. Take it for a ride first?

LINDA: Where to?

BIRDMAN: Wherever you like.

LINDA: The sea?

BIRDMAN: If you want.

LINDA: Come on then.

They get in the car – BIRDMAN turns on the CD player.

AARON: So that's Birdman heading down the river,
Heading for the white bridge and out towards the sea.
If we'd been listening we might have heard him coming.
If we'd been looking we might have seen him smile.

RACHEL: So he scattered his questions over the water.
Who and what and why and why and why
and if we knew we couldn't say.

SITA: But it wasn't our fault.

COLIN: He's not any kind of a hero. So don't think he was
going to help. Or that we're going to help him.

MEL: And don't go thinking that's an end to it all. It's all
just water under the bridge. Things stay the same. If it's
not him, it's someone else. In a while we won't even
remember his name.

SAL: He's just another boy from round here.

AARON: Too late we look and now we see it –
freeze frame.
The silver arrow in the air.
All those questions hanging in the air.
Joey Hawk.
Birdman.
Flies.

The music becomes much louder.
There is the sound of a crash.
Blackout.
Then the sky lights up red.

ROSALIND

A Question of Life

for Franziska and Henry

Thanks to:

Judith Peel and Sarah Peel for talking to me about their experience of being young scientists, Susan Beckett and Fiona Mackie.

I would like to acknowledge how often I have turned to the biographies of Rosalind Franklin by Anne Sayre and, in particular, Brenda Maddox in the writing of this play.

DG

Characters

ESTHER, a young biochemist

JOE, her brother

ROSALIND FRANKLIN

Set A laboratory – but clearly artificial. There are: a couple of chairs; a work-bench; piled up boxes containing props and paraphernalia dating from between the fifties and the present. There is a small area 'off' for the X-ray room.

Notes For playing Wilkins, characters need a jacket. Watson requires a lab-coat.
Rosalind wears a lab-coat with coloured or patterned pockets over a dress.
There are two models of DNA required. Model One is Crick and Watson's incorrect version of DNA. Model Two is the correct version. These do not need to be full-sized. Watson, for example, travelled to America with foot-high versions in perspex cases.
Rosalind is pronounced 'Ros-lind'.
The back wall should be of such a construction that projected images will show up on it.
The breaking of the play into scenes is intended as an aid to rehearsal only – these are not formal breaks.

A note on punctuation A full stop denotes the end of a thought. A comma indicates a thought extending itself. A dash might be thought of as the suspension of a thought, a crystallisation. '/ ' is used to indicate the point at which the next character starts speaking.

Rosalind: A Question of Life was first presented by Birmingham Repertory Theatre on a schools tour on 26 September 2005. The first public performance by Birmingham Repertory Theatre was at the Door on 1 November 2005, by the same company:

ROSALIND, Nicki Walsh
ESTHER, Sheena Irving
JOE, Matthew Barker

Director, Kate Varney
Designer, Oliver Shapley
Lighting Designer, Mike Hurst
Composer, Oliver Searle
Projections, Chris Plant
Technical Stage Manager, Craig Price
Deputy Stage Manager, Darren Abel
Producer, Steve Ball

Scene One

ESTHER enters the space, in the half-dark with her rucksack on her back.

ESTHER: No, no. That's all right. Thanks. I'll sort it out. I can clear (*As she bumps into something.*) myself a space.

The lights come up. ROSALIND is in a chair in the darkness, motionless. ESTHER sees the clutter in the lab.

Where am I going to put all this lot?

She begins to clear a couple of boxes off the work-bench. Then settles down to fire up her computer.

Esther Morgan. Date of birth: 27/6/86.
GCSEs: much the same as everybody else's here.
A levels: good – much the same as everybody else's here.
School attended… Current course…
Special interests: Oh God – they know you make it up, don't they?
Are all your inoculations up to date? What!!
Anything else? How about 'distinguishing marks'? Scar on left arm (from when I fell out of a tree at the age of six), brown stripe in left iris (born that way), double-jointed (it runs in the family). Or…what I had for breakfast?
What does all that tell them? What does that tell them about me, Esther?

There's a knock at the door. ESTHER hears it, but decides not to respond.
There's another knock. Esther's brother, JOE, enters.

JOE: Esther?
What are you doing in here?

ESTHER: How did you find me?

JOE: I asked the caretaker. I told him I was looking for a nerdy girl with glasses. He knew it was you straight away. (–) Joke.

ESTHER: Yeah Joe. Really funny.

JOE: Your phone's off.

ESTHER: Yeah?

JOE: What are you doing in here?

ESTHER: I'm trying to do some work, actually.

JOE: Quiz kid.
What's in all these boxes anyway?

He opens a box and gets out a microscope. Looks through it –

ESTHER: Joe, I really don't think you should be going through them.
This stuff's got nothing to do with us.

JOE: Nobody's been in here for years, have they? How do you…?
(*Focusing the microscope.*) Shit will you look at that. What is it? You ready then?

ESTHER: What do you mean ready? I've got work to do. I just need some quiet to get this done.

JOE: You've forgotten.

ESTHER: Have I?

JOE: You've forgotten.
What's the date?

ESTHER: It's about the fourteenth. The fifteenth? Oh. Oh my God. Dad.

JOE: The penny drops.

Come on. Get your things. I've got the car outside.
Have you got some music?

ESTHER: But I've only just got here. I need to get this done.

JOE: You can do it in the car on the way home. Mum'll be
waiting.

We're not going to leave her on her own tomorrow are we?

ESTHER: I need to fill this in now. It's got to be in
tomorrow. I've got to mail it tonight.

JOE: What is it anyway?

(*He looks at the screen.*)

A job application? That's a bit early isn't it? For a first
year? You're not giving up already are you?

ESTHER: No I am not giving up. It's for a summer job. This
company takes on a couple of students each summer to
work in the office.

JOE: What do they do then?

ESTHER: Oh, research stuff. You know.

JOE: No, I don't know. If I knew I wouldn't be asking would I?
Research into what?

ESTHER: It's genetic research.

JOE: Oh.

ESTHER: There see. I knew it would mean a lot to you.

JOE: No, no it's really interesting. Not.

ESTHER: That's funny. I'd have thought a discussion about
XX chromosomes would have been right up your street.

JOE: That's a bit too deep for me. I'm only interested in the
packaging.

ESTHER: I noticed.

JOE: You're quite prone to a bit of natural selection yourself.

ESTHER: Yeah, well. I'm getting better at it. I've realised it's quality not quantity that counts.

JOE: It's different for blokes. (–) Have you seen Charlie lately?

ESTHER: No. I haven't. And before you ask: I'm not bothered.

JOE: Really not?

ESTHER: Really not.

JOE: Then why are you shut away in here?

ESTHER: I told you: I've got to get on with this. I'm all behind. I didn't realise how much – space – Charlie took up in my head. I let everything go. So when we broke up, I didn't know what I wanted any more. I lost all my sense of direction. Now I've got to catch up.

JOE: How long do you need to fill that in?

ESTHER: However long it takes to make me sound so irresistible they can't turn me down.

JOE: It's just an office job. You'll be taking out the rubbish, making tea.

ESTHER: This year, maybe. Next year or the year after I'll be doing something more important.

JOE: So when I meet another me coming down the street, I'll have you to thank.

ESTHER: Ha ha. Very funny. You read too many comics.

JOE: And please can that Joe keep his hair until he's at least sixty. And I'd like to get more than average exam results.

ESTHER: Firstly: a bald head won't stop you from being the sex god you so clearly are. Secondly: intelligence isn't attached to a single gene. It's much more complicated. You'd do better to turn off that Playstation.
Thirdly: all that cloning babies stuff – that's just a hoax. It's a story, they make it up to sell papers. You know that really.

JOE: Today's hoax. Tomorrow's possibility.

ESTHER: Oh please. There are more important things than pandering to the whims of a few desperate people. It's not about that. Now let me get on, or we'll never get away tonight.

JOE: You think they'll want you?

ESTHER: If I work hard enough.

JOE: Quiz kid.
I'll be back in an hour. Be ready. OK?

ESTHER does not reply.

OK Esther?

ESTHER: OK.

Exit JOE.
ESTHER concentrates on her computer.

Scene Two

ROSALIND lifts a box off her lap and gets up to come down-stage to address the audience. ESTHER cannot hear her.

ROSALIND: I hate small spaces. I've always hated small spaces, so I was no good in the war – air raid shelters, cellars – my nightmare. We spent the day cooped up in labs investigating coal then went out on air raid duty. I was about her age when war broke out.

A life begins at the beginning and ends when it must.
Afterwards: what remains? What remains of me.
With a story you begin at the beginning, but this isn't a story.
Let's say it's an experiment.
The idea, with an experiment, is that afterwards you know a little more than before. You are on your way to finding a truth.

Let's start with the child. It all starts with the child – we forget sometimes.

So – Rosalind, the child. Serious, inevitably. Knitter of some success, but more due to obedience than any true flair, sporty, girl guide wearer of several guiding badges, including morse code.
(*Pause.*)
Sent away to boarding school at the age of nine.
I did not cry.
Much. So that others could see it.
But I did resent it.
I worked.
I wrote letters.
'Dear Mummy and Daddy…'
'Mother and Father dear…'
'How is the new kitten?'
'How is the new baby?'

Hmm.

Boarding-school wasn't for long though. You get over things. Most things.

Some things stick forever.

ROSALIND is quite still again: ESTHER cannot see her.

Scene Three

ESTHER: Oh-oh. Here we go: the million dollar question. I knew it couldn't be that easy. 'Tell us a bit about yourself: why do you want to do this job.' Because taking out the rubbish is good? Making cups of tea is great. Doing science is fantastic.

When I was nine we did a project on Galileo and his life. There was something about him – this man chucking things off the top of the tower of Pisa to see what happens to them – *something* about it all, that made my brain fizz. That you can think like that, that you can *do* that.

There are these forces you can't see, but you know they're there, you can see them at work, and you want to figure things out – what is it, how does it work, if I do this, what happens, if I do that, what happens. And I realised – this is the way my brain works, I like this, I can *feel this*.

It makes me want to dance – these questions, these delicious problems which my mind just wants to attend to. And at the end of it – the beauty of it is – you're heading for the right answer, there is going to be, somewhere, the absolute satisfaction of the right answer – there's going to be a truth at the bottom of it.

And there's all this stuff out there. All these problems waiting to be solved and every day we're moving closer to them. Someone's moving closer to them.

I want to be part of it.

When I was nine, I knew I had to be a scientist.

ROSALIND: Ah yes. Galileo!

ESTHER: Uh! Oh I'm sorry. Where did you come from? I mean I didn't realise there was anybody in here.

ROSALIND: I was just listening to you talking about Galileo. Now there's a man!

ESTHER: You think so?

ROSALIND: Oh yes. You don't think so?

ESTHER: Well, I don't know. I've never thought of him like that. Perhaps. If I'd met him... I'm not really sure he'd be my type.

ROSALIND: Your type?

ESTHER: Well usually I like thin men. You know – moody, intense, a bit troublesome. Unfortunately.

ROSALIND: You don't find their way of thinking the main thing that attracts you to them?

ESTHER: Well, no. Not necessarily.

ROSALIND: I see.
Esther. That's a Jewish name, isn't it?

ESTHER: Yes.

ROSALIND: Are you Jewish?

ESTHER: No. My dad just liked the name.

ROSALIND: Are many of the students here Jewish?

ESTHER: I don't know. I've never asked. No one's ever told me. It's never come up in conversation.

ROSALIND: Really?

ESTHER: Is that good or bad?

ROSALIND: I don't know.

ESTHER: Is it an issue for you?

ROSALIND: It was just a question.

It used to be – an issue – as you call it. For any Jew it had to be.

Who will help? That is what we asked in the war. Who will help? Will you stand up against this terrible abuse of human life, this absurd misuse of scientific argument to justify the notion that one race is inferior to another. Will you help?

For my father it was bitter. He suddenly felt foreign in his own country. He was so thoroughly English. Thoroughly Jewish and thoroughly English. I stood outside his study and heard him crying with anger and disappointment. He was broken apart – all those people needing help, desperately needing help, and he couldn't set enough in motion to save them all.

Such a waste of life.

People trying to leave had to be so – lucky. Little Evi travelled on a train across Europe on her own to come and live with us. She was nine. Imagine that. Nine years old. We were tucked up safe in our own little beds at the age of nine.

ESTHER: The war? You mean – the Second World War?

ROSALIND: Of course.

ESTHER: (*Wants to say, 'You're not old enough…', but can't.*) I'm sorry, I don't know you and we're already half-way through a conversation. The caretaker said this room was empty.

ROSALIND: I'm interrupting you.

ESTHER: I'm in your space.

ROSALIND: Doctor Rosalind Franklin. How do you do.

ESTHER: What shall I call you?

ROSALIND: It'll have to be Rosalind, I'm afraid.

ESTHER: Rosalind. Hi.

ROSALIND: How very American. Hello.

ESTHER: Rosalind.
(*Pause.*)
Have you been here long?

ROSALIND laughs.

I mean – I feel as though I should know you. I think I've heard your name.

ROSALIND: You think you've heard my name?

ESTHER: You're going to tell me you're one of my lecturers and I've missed something. Are you?

ROSALIND: I most definitely am not. Certainly not. I do not teach.

ESTHER: Oh. Well then. I've seen you in the corridor maybe.

ROSALIND: You haven't.

ESTHER: I haven't.

ROSALIND: They're sticky things, first meetings.
Right foot, wrong foot – which one is it going to be?

ESTHER: Rosalind. I'm terribly sorry, but I have to get on with this. It's important. If I'm in your way I can go somewhere else.

ROSALIND: No need. You get on with your work.
I shall get on with mine.
I might need a little help with an experiment. Would you mind?

ESTHER: An experiment? Great! What kind of experiment?

ROSALIND: I'm trying to find out the truth. What remains. Of my life. Of my work. I'd like to see the truth.

Abruptly ROSALIND turns away to get on with her work. ESTHER watches her, then resumes her own work.

Scene Four

ROSALIND clears a box off the work-bench and sets up the microscope. She is preparing a crystal to work with.

ROSALIND: This is my prayer.
A prayer with hardly a breath.
A breath to flow to a steady hand.
The hand that follows the eye
that gives us – clarity.
This is my prayer.
The unknown beam
that shines through the crystal.
The atoms of the crystal diffracting the rays.
A message of life scattered on the photographic plate.

Scene Five

ROSALIND has been working for a long time. There's a knock at the door. It's JOE as Wilkins.

ROSALIND: (*Waves him in without looking up.*) Come!

JOE / WILKINS: Hello there! Welcome to King's College. I suppose I should say welcome back to London and welcome to King's. Do you know the university at all? Something of a change from Paris, I expect.

He goes to shake her hand, she does not remove it from the microscope.

Oh sorry. Maurice Wilkins. DNA's my area. My lab's
just down the corridor. I thought I'd pop along and
introduce myself.

ROSALIND is still not reacting.

Sorry I wasn't here to get you started.
Where have you set up the camera is it through…?

*He goes to pull back the curtain to the X-ray room, but
ROSALIND's glare stops him from going in.*

I can see you're all ready. You have got everything
haven't you? (–) Jolly good. Jolly good.
(–) I'll be in and out from now on. (–)
Well. Let me know when you've got a decent photograph.

ROSALIND: Why?

JOE / WILKINS: Well I shall need to see it. I'm eager to see
it. The idea is that it'll be useful. It'll speed us up. Things
have been moving slowly.
(*He can't hold her gaze.*)
Obviously.

ROSALIND lets the conversation dry up. JOE / WILKINS leaves.

ROSALIND: As first meetings go – not a huge success. What
are the facts: An introduction. A meeting. An apology.
A declaration of intent: to be 'in and out from now on'.
And an order.
What's in there, between the lines?
That one person is taking charge of another's work.
That's what.

*There's a knock at the door. It's JOE / WILKINS again. He's
got chocolates.*

But he is persistent. Like mist or damp or a little dog.
Scratching at my door again.

JOE / WILKINS: Rosalind. I wondered. If perhaps you would like to come to tea? In the common room?

He holds out the chocolates. She doesn't take them. She doesn't take her eyes off him. He does not hold eye contact.

ROSALIND: Thank you Maurice. I'm sure you're aware the common room is not open to women.

JOE / WILKINS: I meant the joint common room – we could have tea in the joint. With the others. Have a talk over tea. Exchange – pleasantries. Some chat – about work. That kind of thing. I see.
(*He has to put the chocolates down.*)
No.

ROSALIND: I have already had tea. 'Pleasantries' I find frankly tedious. I must get on with my work. My own work. I take it seriously, as you can see. Maurice.

JOE / WILKINS: Rosalind I really think /

ROSALIND: Shut the door when you go Maurice.

JOE / WILKINS turns away. ROSALIND puts her head on the desk. Exasperated. Exhausted.

He can't even look me in the eye.
I think I hate it here.
(*She sits up again.*)
I also tried. We went out.

JOE / WILKINS comes back, they move and sit glumly, eating the chocolates.

JOE / WILKINS: That was jolly good cream.

ROSALIND: But it was not real cream.

(*Silence.*)

It's a good year for mushrooms.

Silence. She and JOE / WILKINS look at each other for a moment.

Scene Six

JOE takes off the jacket, completely puzzled.

JOE: (*To ESTHER.*) Did I just come in wearing this?

ESTHER: Yes.

JOE: No. What. What is this?

ROSALIND: London University. King's College.

ESTHER: Joe, I think it's an – experiment.

JOE: An experiment??

ESTHER: I don't know what else to call it.

JOE: Who's your friend?

ESTHER: Doctor Rosalind Franklin.

JOE: Doctor who?

ESTHER: Rosalind Franklin.

JOE: Never heard of her. What's going on? What kind of an experiment?

ESTHER: I'm not sure. She said: 'to find out what remains'. That's what she said.

JOE: I mean will you look at the way she's dressed. What time is it? I mean what year?

ESTHER: Some time. Our time. Her time. Never. Just go with it. Please.

Scene Seven

ROSALIND: So much depends, so much depends on the first meeting.
How does this person think? Is there going to be stimulating conversation? Is it going to be fun? Will it last?

ESTHER: You should invite him to dinner.

JOE: What me?

ESTHER: No, Maurice Wilkins. Are you – Were you any good at cooking?

ROSALIND: I'm a chemist. It's all about molecules. Of course I'm good at cooking.
I did not invite him to dinner.
I had given up so much to come here. Paris. Paris!
My friends. People I cared about. People I… People I missed.
(*Pause.*)
People I could work well with.
I was so happy there.
You must understand – I really wanted this to work out.

After the war we were all excited about LIFE.
So much of science in the war had been about death.
With the help of science it had become possible to kill thousands of people in a matter of seconds.
It had become possible and it had been done.
Thousands of people had died in the blink of an eye, the split of an atom.
We did not want that.

We wanted our science to be – unequivocally good – to be of benefit, to be science of life, not science of death. We were full of excitement.

I wanted this job to be good – it was the problem I needed. I started out in London, investigating carbon, then I went to Paris. I learnt how to use diffraction techniques – that's using X-rays to photograph crystals. And so this was my next step. To use X-ray crystallography to study the chemistry of organic matter. It was something new.

It was a challenge.

It was the opportunity to shine the light on life.

(*Getting angry.*) And then he – Wilkins, wanted to take it away. Can you see that? Do you understand? He thought he was in charge of my work. He thought I was an assistant! His assistant. He thought I was going to deliver the photographs and he was going to analyse them! I had given up so much in Paris to come here.

JOE: Can I just say something here?

ROSALIND: If it's relevant. If it's got something to do with the facts.

JOE: What's bitten you? You're in such a rage. If there's a problem, why don't you just sort the problem? You're a bunch of scientists – a bunch of brains – why can't you just divide the labour up, agree to keep out of each other's way?

ROSALIND: I am out of his way! Why can't he just stay out of mine and leave me alone! I've been brought here to work on DNA and that's what I'm going to do. I've come here to *work*.

He should get back to his microscopes and let me get on.

ESTHER: Did you say that to him?

ROSALIND: Not exactly. No. It had to be sorted by the head of the lab. We couldn't agree on anything.

Even without speaking to each other, we could not agree on anything. We were – what – mutually repellent?

ESTHER: Bad chemistry.

ROSALIND: What is that? Something chemical? What starts bad chemistry?

ESTHER: I don't know.

ROSALIND: Is it because I am a woman? Because I'm Jewish? Because I'm from a different class? Or because he is…a disappointment.
All those men meeting in the pub to…talk.
I have a research assistant, Raymond Gosling, but it doesn't seem fair to involve him in all this.

I have no one to talk to.

Half the brilliance of science is in asking the right question – that's what steers you to the heart of the problem.

JOE: And you didn't ask?

ROSALIND: We couldn't communicate.

Scene Eight

ROSALIND: I worked.
(*She takes up her work again.*)
What is it about work that is so – soothing.
Doing science is a quiet place inside of me.

You have to leave behind feeling ruffled, feeling upset, thinking about other people, missing people… Missing them.

There is just – the hand and the eye, the crystal and the ray, the ray and the crystal, the eye and the hand.
(*She takes a jar of DNA.*)
Look at this. This Signer DNA is tremendous stuff. Marvellous. The best there is. I can pull it out into long strings, take a single fibre and set it up in the X-ray.

She takes the slide through to the X-ray room.

ESTHER: That's dangerous. Where's your lead apron?

ROSALIND: (*Coming back.*) Aprons!

ESTHER: But you must have known it was dangerous. You knew it was dangerous.

ROSALIND: When we are young we think we are – invincible.

JOE: No. Not all of us. Some of us know we aren't.

ROSALIND: Aprons. Perhaps we were – I was – thoughtless there. That's true. You don't want to believe that what you are closely connected to is going to turn against you. These rays – were our friends. For some of us they held a promise to unlock so many secrets. The key to making the invisible visible.
We were thoughtless, perhaps.

ESTHER: Obsessed.

ROSALIND: I've heard that before.

JOE: It's arrogant to think that you are bigger than the things you are playing with.

ROSALIND: Absolutely. What did Galileo say:
'Anyone who had experienced just once the perfect understanding of one single thing, and had truly tasted how knowledge is accomplished, would recognise that infinity of other truths of which he understands nothing.'

JOE: And that means?

ESTHER: Science is never finished.

ROSALIND: I spend my days straining to see things which cannot be seen, looking for the universe reflected in a cell.

JOE: What? I don't understand. I thought you were taking X-ray photographs of crystals. What are you doing with them?

ROSALIND: Am I wasting my time here?

JOE: Oh, hang on a minute. I'm just her brother. I don't know what I've wandered into here. I'm just doing what I'm told. I'm not a scientist. I don't even know what I'm doing.

ROSALIND: I can tell.

ESTHER: He only asked a question. It was an honest question.

ROSALIND: We're investigating DNA. The molecular structure of DNA.
When we have a photograph. *When*. It's not easy taking photographs. The first challenge is to get the crystal. You have to obtain a good crystal before you can even begin to take the photograph.

JOE: And once you have it, then…?

ROSALIND: The X-ray beam is shone into the vacuum and channelled through the crystal. The atoms of the crystal diffract the beam – send them off at different angles

– so the flecks of light on the photographic plate are not a true image – the scientist's job is to interpret those flecks, to reconstruct the molecule. The photograph is like a distorted map. You have to apply equations – there's a lot of maths involved. You have to be able to think in three dimensions.

(*Lecturing increasingly rapidly here, until it's like a machine gun – she wanders off, might even have her back to JOE and us.*)
Our results suggest a helical structure (which must be very closely packed) containing probably two, three or four co-axial nucleic acid chains per helical unit, and having the phosphate groups near the outside.
Did you get that?

JOE shrugs. ROSALIND doesn't react to it.

JOE: Why don't you just make a model?

ROSALIND: (*Furious.*) You make a model once you've got your experimental data. What are you going to make a model of if you don't have any clues??

JOE: Easy tiger. All I said was /

ROSALIND: I heard what you said. You want to play. You're just not serious about this. You can't make a model without any facts. It's absurd.

ESTHER: But there are models. I've seen them. Those other scientists, Watson and Crick, made models. I saw it in a book.

ROSALIND: You make the model once you've got your data – hard facts. It's not conjured out of thin air. You have to experiment. You have to know the dimensions, the possibilities of spacing, what likes to go with what – what repels, what attracts. You can't just guess. Not *all* of it. Unless you're some kind of genius. You need some evidence to go on.

She sees JOE looking at her blankly. ROSALIND returns to her corner. She's exasperated, trying to find calm in her work again.

I'm surrounded here by people who are not serious. By men who are playing. People who don't have the first idea about chemical bonds. It's infuriating.
It's exhausting me. I've been locked up in here for weeks. I can't go on any longer.

ESTHER: I think you need a holiday.

ROSALIND: I do. I do. I can't wait to get away.
But models without data just go wrong. Let me show you. Where is that first model of Watson and Crick's? It's here somewhere. Which box is it in? Let me just…

ROSALIND searching through some boxes – can't find what she wants. JOE finds a box, lifts out Model One.

Scene Nine

JOE: Here it is!

ROSALIND: American.

JOE: What?

ROSALIND: It's all right, what you're doing, but you have to be American.
Jim Watson is American.

JOE: *(As JOE.)* Do I need the jacket?

He picks up the black jacket.

ROSALIND: Not that one. That's Maurice Wilkins.

JOE: I think I need something.

ROSALIND: Watson and Crick didn't wear lab-coats. It's historically inaccurate. But look at your clothes! You don't look right, it's true. Here take this one.

ROSALIND thrusts a lab-coat at him.

JOE / WATSON: Well, what do you think?

ROSALIND is walking round the model.

ESTHER: I'm absolutely lost now. We're in America? What are we doing in America?

ROSALIND: Oh for goodness' sake. Cambridge. We're in Cambridge now. You really haven't got very far with your research on DNA have you? Watson and Crick are working at the Cavendish Institute at Cambridge University.

ESTHER: So he's Watson?

ROSALIND: That's right, James Watson. He's American.

ESTHER: Why does he get all the best parts? Aren't there any women in this?

ROSALIND: Not here, no.

ESTHER: You mean you're the only woman?

ROSALIND: In this part of the story.

ESTHER: There are no women around at all?

ROSALIND: Not on this project. There are very few of us, you understand.
Science really isn't considered an accomplishment in a woman.

ESTHER: Loads of women do science now. Just loads.
But you weren't really on your own, were you? There

were women at Cambridge after the war. Science
undergraduates. Research graduates.

JOE / WATSON: You can forget them. I want a girl. Not a
scientist.
I want popsies. Nothing complicated. Some girl. Blonde.
Who's going to let me unbutton her blouse. Not one
who's going to make like she's thinking and break my
balls in the process.

ROSALIND: See.

ESTHER: Was Watson really like that? 'I want a girl not a
scientist.' What kind of shit is that?

JOE: (*As JOE.*) It's in the interests of collecting the evidence.
That's all. What's the big deal?

ROSALIND: It might have been a little strong. The last bit.
He might not have expressed himself so – vividly.

ESTHER: Is that what *you* really think Joe? You and all your
mates?

ROSALIND: Just ignore it.

ESTHER: But it's not fair.

ROSALIND: We're doing my story now.

ESTHER: But how do you put up with it?

ROSALIND: You're a *scientist.*
You have to ignore it or you won't get anywhere.
You can't allow yourself to think about it, you can't
listen to that little voice – 'What do they think of me,
what do they think of me, what do they think of me.
What are they talking about behind the closed door.'
(*Pause.*)
You have to concentrate on the science, focus on that.

Do your job. Ignore the rest. Don't enter into it. You'll never get used to it, but you have to learn to be strong. It's about the science.

ESTHER is subdued.

It's just for now. This part of my life. It won't always be like this. Look. Trust me.

ESTHER: I still haven't got a part.

ROSALIND: You can be Crick. He's a friend of Maurice Wilkins. Francis Crick.

ESTHER: American?

ROSALIND: No. English. Loud. Brilliant.

ESTHER: Is he into popsies too?

JOE: Well of course he is. Who wouldn't be – given the choice?

ROSALIND: He is married.

JOE: So?

ESTHER shoots him a look.

ESTHER: What am I doing?

She puts on a lab-coat.

ROSALIND: It's your model – yours and Watson's – I'm here with Wilkins. We've come from London, from the lab at King's, to see it.

JOE and ESTHER get ready to be in character, to exchange welcomes and pleasantries before their great unveiling.

ESTHER / CRICK: How do you do. How was the journey? I hear /

ROSALIND: Can we see it now?

She has caught JOE and ESTHER off guard. They turn to
the model. ROSALIND circles the model examining it.

JOE: Well? What do you think?

ROSALIND: Where's the water?
You're building models and you ignore the hard facts.
I distinctly stated that the magnesium ions holding the
phosphate groups together have to be surrounded by
tight shells of water molecules. Where are they? Are
they – hiding?

No don't tell me – you've got some pretty little theory
about where they are hiding, haven't you?
No?

And you've got the sugar-phosphate backbone going
down the centre. That won't work. The sugar-phosphate
backbone has to be on the outside. I gave you that
deduction in my lecture. You were there, weren't you
listening? There's no point in coming to these things if
you're not going to pay attention.

Unless of course you're just playing.

It just doesn't hold up does it?

Maurice – did you say there was a train at twenty to four?

ROSALIND does a grand sweep 'out' and comes downstage.
JOE / WATSON and ESTHER / CRICK are left crushed.

JOE / WATSON: Nice to meet you, Rosy.
What did I say about ball-breakers?
No wonder Wilkins sounds so depressed.

ESTHER / CRICK: Why didn't you write that down when
you went to her lecture?

JOE / WATSON: (*Shrugs.*) I wasn't listening.

ESTHER and JOE remove their lab-coats.

ESTHER: Oh my God, what was that?

JOE: Now you know how it feels.

ESTHER: But she's right about the model though. You need data. She is right, isn't she?

Behind ROSALIND's back. ESTHER sits down at the computer and begins to work. Types in: 'DNA structure'. Searches. Photo 51 comes up – it appears on the screen behind.

Scene Ten

There's a sense of outside.

ROSALIND: At the foot of the mountain – at the foot of the mountain you are filled with excitement at the prospect of the journey to the peak. You know – you hope – it will be arduous, precarious, dangerous, stretch you to the very limit. Until your bones crack. But you want to get there – more than anything you want to see the world spread out before you. You want to have *made it.*

It's the journey, the effort, that counts. To arrive at the summit without the experience of getting there – that would be to arrive without blood pumping through your veins, without the sharper sight of constant wariness, without the sweet pain of overworked muscles. You create it – it's your own climb, your own pain, your own victory. As I get nearer to the top – I don't look down, I don't look across to see how the stranger on the nearby rock-face is doing. I give my full concentration to the mountain.
It is the mountain and me.

The instant summit – that would be nothing more than a picture postcard – it wouldn't be mine, my own.

In France. It was cold. We set out in cloud. And suddenly, quite suddenly, at sunrise the cloud lifted, just as we were coming out onto the glacier. There were pink summits above a sea of cloud. The light rested so gently on the mountains and on the clouds. I was so happy. I had to weep. The world is so beautiful.

ESTHER: Joe. Joe – what's this? Have I pressed something I shouldn't have? I can't get rid of this.

JOE also comes over to look at the computer.

JOE: You've just got to click here. No. Uh. Try again. Uh. No. What is this?

Photo 51 keeps coming back. They can't erase it.

ROSALIND: (*Still out front.*) It is so beautiful.

ESTHER: What is this? Rosalind, did you take this photograph? Rosalind?

Scene Eleven

ROSALIND: I could stay here forever.

ESTHER: Rosalind?

ROSALIND: Mm.
(*She hears Wilkins' voice calling her back from far away.*)
Maurice.

She goes to the desk and picks up Photo 51.

ESTHER: Joe – she thinks I'm Maurice Wilkins. Give me his jacket.

She moves to take it.

JOE: But I do Wilkins. You do Crick.

ESTHER: I'm doing Wilkins this time. You stick with Watson.

She gets the jacket.

ROSALIND: (*Absorbed in Photo 51.*) This is helical. It looks helical. But where's the evidence?

She gets up. Restless. Places Photo 51 in a pile of papers. She is drawn back to her work, picks up a jar of DNA to take into the X-ray room, moves away from her desk and crosses the stage to address the audience.
As she speaks, ESTHER / WILKINS crosses to ROSALIND's work-place and takes up the pile of papers.

I am leaving this place.
I'm going to walk out of here.
I've heard Wilkins is going to repeat my experiments. It will be as though I'd never been. I shall disappear from this place without a trace.

What am I left with? – I'm forbidden to even *think* about DNA when I leave here.
Like a thoroughly naughty girl.
The nasty girl.
But they're right, of course.
You give up a job, you give up a problem. It's a job. Not your life.
Although it might feel as though it's your life.
But it's so hard to stop thinking about something.
At Birkbeck, I'm moving on to work at Birkbeck College, there will be a new delicious problem.
And it must be better there than here.
The signs are good – more foreigners, more Jews. I might feel more at home. Away from this underground

cell. It feels like a tomb. I just want to get out into the light. I have to get on.

ROSALIND goes into the X-ray room with the jar.
ESTHER / WILKINS moves away from ROSALIND's desk
with the pile of papers.

Scene Twelve

JOE enters swiftly as Watson.

JOE / WATSON: You should collaborate you know, Maurice.

ESTHER / WILKINS: Who with? With you? But you're not working on DNA any more.
Are you? Are you? DNA belongs to us. It's King's problem. That was agreed.

JOE / WATSON: (*Does not answer.*) You should collaborate. The Americans are going to find it if you don't get a move on. It's a race on the final straight.

ESTHER / WILKINS: Rosy says she's leaving. I've been working on this for a very long time. Another month is neither here nor there. I'm not rushing into anything. Once she's gone I'll get down to work. More haste, less speed Jim. Do you know that proverb?

He's looking at Photo 51.

JOE / WATSON: You really should collaborate you know.

ESTHER / WILKINS: Will you look here. What's she called this? (*He turns the photo over to look at the back.*)
Photo 51. This photograph really is very good you know. It's really quite beautiful.

JOE / WATSON takes the photo, looks, then gives it back.

JOE / WATSON: Hm.

ESTHER / WILKINS goes back to ROSALIND's work-place to put Photo 51 back. JOE turns away in his barely suppressed excitement.

JOE / WATSON: Holy Moses! Holy cow! It is a helix! It's definitely a helix.

He makes some quick notes on a newspaper.

ESTHER / WILKINS: It is very good isn't it?

JOE / WATSON: Maurice. (*Shoving the newspaper in his pocket.*) Afraid I have to go now. I'm – playing tennis this evening.

ESTHER / WILKINS: I thought we could have tea in the common room. I could introduce you to the other chaps. We could go to the pub afterwards.

JOE / WATSON: Sorry. I forgot. Prior engagement. You know.

ESTHER / WILKINS: Ah. She's important obviously.

JOE / WATSON: Who?

ESTHER / WILKINS: This woman you're playing tennis with.

JOE / WATSON: Ah. Yes. Yes. She could be.

They part. ESTHER takes off Wilkins' jacket. ROSALIND comes back from the X-ray room.

ROSALIND: I shall be so glad to leave this place.

ESTHER: But you can't leave. You're nearly there! This photo /

ROSALIND: I can't quite find it. I can't quite see it. Time is running out and I've got to write this up. I can't leave it in a mess for Gosling.

ESTHER: Your assistant? Should I be Gosling?

She goes to get the lab-coat.

ROSALIND: We're working.

ESTHER: If I were Gosling, I could persuade you. Talk you into / staying.

ROSALIND: Nobody talks me into anything.
I'm leaving.
I'm working.

ESTHER: (*Lets the lab-coat drop.*) Why don't you just stop, just for a minute? And listen? You're close to it. You are. What if somebody else finds it?

ROSALIND: Somebody else *will* find it. It's there to be found. I'm not staying now. My mind is made up. I have to leave.

ESTHER: And what if Wilkins finds it?

ROSALIND: I will still have been part of it. He will have all my work. Gosling is still here. And my report with all my findings has already gone. I'm all ready to go.

She loses herself in her notebook.

ESTHER: Rosalind? Rosalind?

Scene Thirteen

ESTHER and JOE are lost, waiting. ESTHER goes back to her computer. JOE starts to go through boxes.

JOE: Hey, Es – look at this.
(*He takes a mechanical fish out of a box. He winds it up and watches it flap its fins. Winds it again.*)
Brilliant. Dad would really have liked this. He would have had a laugh with this.

ESTHER: You could take it.

JOE: You've changed your tune. You said I shouldn't be going through these boxes.

ESTHER: Yeah but – we're part of this now. And nobody's going to reclaim lost property fifty years on, are they? And it's not exactly bursting with scientific significance, is it?

JOE: Is that the only thing that matters? 'Scientific significance?' Somebody *chose* this. They might have chosen it to give to someone, to give them a laugh. Or to say sorry or something.

ESTHER: Put it on dad's grave tomorrow.

JOE: Do you think he'll see it?

ESTHER: I think it would make you feel better.
Mum'll like it. They were always laughing, weren't they? At least, in my head they were always laughing.

JOE: Yeah, they were.

ESTHER: He was all right, wasn't he. As a dad, I mean?

JOE: Yeah.

ESTHER: (*On her computer.*) I need two referees for this: shall I put down my old chemistry teacher? Is he a good idea? One of them should be somebody who's known me for a couple of years. Do you think he'll be all right?

JOE: – Esther – this job you're going to do. I don't think you should do it.

ESTHER: Joe, you're just like everyone else – you hear the word 'genetics' and all you can think about is cloning human beings. I told you: it's *not* about cloning human beings. We're not allowed to do that. It's illegal.

JOE: But they just have. On the news they said – they'd done it, cloned human embryos.

ESTHER: Embryonic cells. It's just a bundle of cells – right at the very beginning. It's a bundle of totipotent cells. Ones that can grow into any kind of human cell – the same as the donor. So we'll be able to use them for the donor and they won't be rejected. It's fantastic Joe – fantastic science.

JOE: Yeah. Great.

ESTHER: No need to sound so enthusiastic. It's not the same as a drive-by on *Grand Theft Auto* obviously. But for scientists, it is the next level.

JOE: But don't you ever think about what it means – creating life. Are you sure about it?

ESTHER: You mean: playing God.

JOE: Or Frankenstein.

ESTHER: But it's not a life, is it? It's before a life.

JOE: But somehow the spark's there isn't it? You've made this living thing.

ESTHER: It won't be allowed to develop. It's not a life.

JOE: But these cells are dividing – you set it off, zap zap zap – and then it's got its own momentum – it's going to keep going, if you don't stop it. Doesn't that make you think at all?

ESTHER: No. It couldn't keep going – it's not implanted in a womb.

JOE: But what if somebody did do that – implanted it in a womb?

ESTHER: Look Joe. It's just a bundle of cells. It's not a baby. It doesn't have a heart or a brain or limbs or anything. It's just a few cells and it won't be allowed to develop beyond that. It's nothing to be afraid of.

JOE: But don't you ever ask yourself where a life starts? Are we just bundles of cells or are we something more than that? Hm? When I think about dad /

ESTHER: Look Joe, I know it's the anniversary tomorrow, but maybe you think about dad too much.

JOE: Well today you'd forgotten him.
He wouldn't want you to do this.

ESTHER: I think he would. He'd want me to go forward. He'd want to be proud of me.

JOE: You just want to be a winner, don't you? You want to be the champion quiz kid. You want to be like that boy.

ESTHER: What boy?

JOE: You know. Quiz kid boy.

ESTHER: SHUT UP Joe!

Scene Fourteen

ROSALIND: (*Distracted from her work.*) Mmh? What's this? Is this noise really necessary?

JOE: Quiz kids. The school competition – for all the boffins, you know. Clever questions for clever kids.

JOE goes into 'quizmaster' mode:

JOE / QUIZMASTER: First round.

ESTHER: No Joe, don't.

JOE: First round.

ESTHER is still uncooperative.

It's an experiment. My experiment. (*To ROSALIND.*) Let's all do it. You be the boy.

He pushes ESTHER into position. She and ROSALIND are facing each other. ESTHER reacts as a girl of fourteen; ROSALIND as the boy.

Do it.

JOE / QUIZMASTER: First round: Who discovered the moons of Jupiter?

ESTHER: Galileo.

JOE / QUIZMASTER: Who discovered the world's first Ichthyosaur at the age of twelve?

ROSALIND / BOY: Mary Anning.

JOE / QUIZMASTER: In which year did Aldous Huxley write *Brave New World*?
Was it a)1932; b)1967; or c)1972?

ESTHER: Could you repeat the question please?

JOE / QUIZMASTER: Which year did Aldous Huxley write *Brave New World*? 1932, 1967 or 1972?

ESTHER: 1932.

JOE / QUIZMASTER: Who was the first woman to win a Nobel Prize?

ROSALIND / BOY: Marie Curie.

JOE / QUIZMASTER: In 1964 she was the first British woman to win a Nobel Prize – who was she?

ESTHER: Dorothy Crowfoot Hodgkin.

JOE / QUIZMASTER: The father of modern genetics published his paper on heredity in 1865 – who was he?

ROSALIND / BOY: Gregor Mendel.

JOE / QUIZMASTER: Name the author of *Frankenstein*.

There's a pause. ESTHER is looking around at the audience. Is she searching for something?

Who was the author of Frankenstein? No whispering in the audience please.
You must know the story of the man-made monster brought to life with a flash of electricity? No idea? Come on you must know this one. Go on – make a guess. You've got nothing to lose. Everything to gain by making a guess.

ESTHER: I don't know.

JOE / QUIZMASTER: Don't know? You don't know. Over to you.
(*To ROSALIND / BOY.*) Who was the author of *Frankenstein* ?

ROSALIND / BOY: (*Triumphantly.*) Mary Shelley!

JOE: (*Disgusted.*) This boy won it.

ESTHER: He did win it.

ESTHER walks away.

JOE: And now you want to be like him. Anything to win it.

ESTHER shrugs.

ROSALIND: That was – exhilarating. Just exhilarating. (*Then she realises:*) I'm shaking. Look at me, I'm all shaky. (*She makes a deliberate effort to regain her composure.*) (*To JOE, briskly again, in charge.*) Interesting. A good experiment. Were you a quiz kid too?

JOE: Me? No way. Not my thing. It was clear that nerdy kid was going to win – he was way out there.

ROSALIND: Except for Esther. She was 'way out there' too?

JOE: Oh sure. Except for Esther. But I knew she wasn't going to win.

ROSALIND: Why not?

JOE shrugs.

Why not?

JOE: I'm her brother.
You could see it. You could smell it. That kid wasn't even aware of the world around him, he wanted to win that much. All those people sitting in the hall, holding their breath, waiting for the answer. Waiting for him to slip up. He couldn't even see us.
He didn't care what we thought. He was just heading straight for it. Because he wanted to win. It never crossed his mind he wasn't going to win. And now she wants to be like him.

ESTHER: I flunked it, Joe. But not because of that boy.
I lost my concentration. I was too tired or something. Somebody coughed. And it was you, Joe.
You coughing. And then I looked. And you looked just like dad – and I felt this terrible – whoosh – I missed dad. It went right through me.
It's funny how things flash through your mind sometimes – how quickly you can think – like three films at once, all playing at once. I thought so many things in thirty seconds – I remembered when I said I wanted to be a scientist at tea one day. And they laughed and said – you could be a doctor. That'd be good, a doctor in the family. And I said – no – I want to

be a research scientist – work in a lab, do experiments. And dad said – it will be useful, won't it? Is that useful? And you sat there in the audience, coughing just like dad, and I couldn't believe he'd gone. It was like he was in the room. And then I remembered coming home from school, and gran was sitting there crying. And I'd never seen her cry before. And it was all creepy quiet. No radio. She always had the radio on. Crying for her boy. My dad. He'd had a massive asthma attack and his heart had given way. His poor heart. And then you came home and she had to tell it all over again. And it didn't change, the way she told it – it was like – she couldn't find any other words to say it. There just aren't any other words.

My boy, she said. My boy.

And so – when I heard you coughing I just suddenly missed dad. And it was quiet around me, I was far away. And I didn't care about winning. I just really didn't care. I just wanted dad back.

JOE: I didn't know that. You never told me that.
But don't you see – now you want to be like that boy, the boy who wins.

ESTHER: I want to help find something.
It's not about fame, is it?

ROSALIND: You're very sure about that.

ESTHER: You want to be part of the winning team – but in the end it's about finding the answer. That's what matters. Not fame. It's about solving the problem.

ROSALIND: But it does rankle, not doing as well as you could. Letting yourself down – that's hard.
You don't like to give up. It's not what we do.
But sometimes, when you're in a corner, when you've

been forced into a corner, you just can't do your work.
It's impossible.
And then – you have to leave.
I had to leave.

ROSALIND goes into the X-ray room.

JOE: I've got to get out of here.

ESTHER: But I haven't finished. We still don't have the whole story. I want to know how it all fits together. We're in this – situation – there's something going on here, something extraordinary – and you're tired of the wallpaper. You just want something new all the time, don't you? Flick the switch, change the channel, get onto the next level. What do you think the next level is here? Where do you think this is going?

JOE shrugs.

It's just not your game, is it?
You'd think we might have similar interests, somehow, just a bit, wouldn't you? We grew up together. We've got the same parents. But we're really not alike at all.
Sometimes I think you come from a different planet.
I don't get it.

Scene Fifteen

JOE angrily kicks a box – Model Two falls out – dislocated.

JOE: Shit. I've broken it. Did she hear that?

ESTHER: Well let's see what you can do with that then.

JOE is desperately trying to put the model back together. But he hasn't got a clue.

JOE: Well I don't know do I?
  You're the one that's supposed to be a scientist.
  Don't you know how it goes? Have you been paying
  attention?

ESTHER: Let me have a look. Is it the same as the other
  one? No. Look it's got the sugar-phosphate backbone
  down the outside, just like she said it should, and the
  chains go in opposite directions – one up, one down.
  No, don't untwist that – they said it's got to be a helix
  – that's what the photo showed us.

JOE: What about these?

ESTHER: Um. Let me think: the base pairs – how does it go
  – Uh: 'A goes to T, G goes to C.' Adenine and thymine
  go together, guanine goes with cytosine.

  ESTHER helps JOE put the base pairs into place.

JOE: Is that it?

ESTHER: Yeah. That's it. That is it! The double helix. It's all
  in place.

JOE: You're sure that's right?

ESTHER: Yeah. I think so.
  Oh God I see it now. I understand – look: It's like a zip
  – when these chains separate – you've got the bases that
  are going to find the opposite ones to their pair – so you
  recreate the whole thing again. Do you see? Divide and
  complete, split and reform, separate and recreate…over
  and over and over and over. That's it! That is it: DNA!

  It's kind of beautiful, isn't it?

JOE: Beautiful? Yeah. If you say so. Why?

ESTHER: Oh Joe – you don't understand it at all do you?
That's the shape of life.
It contains the genetic code.
That's what makes us how we are. Every cell. Us. Every
one of us different. Unique.
That's the answer to our heredity there. Our history
written in four letters. And it's the key to our future.
I love science – you find the solution to one problem
and a whole new set of problems appears.

JOE: Yeah?

ESTHER: Mapping the genome. Pre-implantation
diagnostics. Cell therapy. Because of this, we can begin
to do all that.
It's like this is the beginning of the next level.

JOE: Does she know that?

ESTHER: I don't know. I shouldn't think so. She's never
talked of it, has she? She's only interested in that
notebook.

ROSALIND: (*Has turned her attention to them and now comes
over to look at the model.*)
You found it! You've got it!
It still takes my breath away.
From all sides. From all sides it looks good. It looks true.
Everything is in place.
It is true.
Congratulations! Go on, Esther. You can be Watson and
stride around waving a piece of paper.

ESTHER: Watson?

JOE: It's your line – the one you want

ESTHER: Which line?

JOE: You know – 'I've got it, we've got it!'

ROSALIND: (*Begins to rummage through boxes.*) That's the one. I've got a bottle of something special in one of these boxes somewhere. Did you see it when you were going through them?
What's in here? No.
(*She sees the fish.*)
Oh you found the fish! Oh. So long ago. What's in this one?
(*It's full of evaporation dishes.*)
Oh, I don't know. Do you want coffee?

JOE: Can't we go to the pub?

ROSALIND: I can't. You go if you like. I've got work to do.

ROSALIND moves away to her desk to pick up Photo 51.

Scene Sixteen

ROSALIND: (*Very excited and going into a tunnel of deep thought, forgetting ESTHER and JOE.*) Marvellous. It was just marvellous.
Everything fell into place. It all made sense.
All our experimental data, the sugar-phosphate backbone, the water, it was all in that model.
It was so pretty – the way it all fell into place.
I was happy – I had been on the right track. I had been thinking along the right lines.
We all knew everyone was going to get very excited about the model. And Photo 51 supported it absolutely.
How beautifully it all fitted together.

ESTHER: What do you mean *fitted*? Of course it fits. *Of course it does*, Rosalind.
Your data and the evidence of Photo 51 were vital to help them get there.

ROSALIND: What?

ESTHER: I said: Photo 51 was a vital clue.

ROSALIND: No no. You're mistaken.

ESTHER: I am not mistaken. We saw it.
Wilkins showed Watson Photo 51. We saw it. It was part of the experiment.

ROSALIND: What do you mean Wilkins showed Watson Photo 51? I didn't know that. Nobody asked me. Nobody told me. Are you sure?

ESTHER: I'm sure.

ROSALIND: I didn't see it. Why didn't I see it?

JOE: Watson did say you should collaborate.

ROSALIND: But I was working on my own. There were no partners. Who was I supposed to collaborate with? He didn't tell us he was working on DNA again, did he?

JOE: You should have shared the photograph.

ROSALIND: Every scientist has a right to evaluate their own evidence before they share it with others! I was just getting ready to speak.

JOE: But if you'd shared /

ROSALIND: Oh, if if if if if if IF. That's not very scientific, is it? I was playing by the rules.

JOE: Well it looks as though sometimes you win first, then you decide whether the rules matter or not.

ROSALIND: It wasn't a race. I didn't know I was in a race with them.

JOE: And so now you're an also-ran.

ROSALIND: An also-ran. My name. My *work*. What becomes of my work?

ESTHER: Try not to take it so personally.

ROSALIND: It feels deeply personal.

JOE: You said you wouldn't care if someone else found it.

ROSALIND: You want the problem to be solved.
But I didn't know my work was helping their discovery. Why hide that? Why? Isn't the discovery big enough? Look – many people contribute to a discovery. All the time we take what somebody else has found out, and use that as a stepping-stone to making our own discovery. We help each other. Progress is a joint effort. But it's fundamental for science that every scientist acknowledges the help they get from others. If we don't do that – if we begin to keep secrets, we won't be able to trust each other. Nobody will share their work. Nobody.

ESTHER: But didn't you have the slightest suspicion?

ROSALIND: I have to believe what another truth-seeker tells me. That they tell the whole truth, not a half-truth. That the work is bigger than the scientist's need to be famous.

JOE: I can't believe you didn't see it coming. You must have been asleep.

ROSALIND: I was not asleep!
I had my eye on my work. Only that. Only that. I missed it. I wasn't looking. I missed it. Just as I missed the answer.
(*ROSALIND storms off down front.*)
Sometimes a fog falls
up a steep face
on a sheer edge.

It's sheer. It's steep.
In a pair, with a friend, you call out:
Move, move.
Be still.
Inch by inch.
Move, move.
Here, it's here.
Hold tight.
Move, move.
You have to move.
Trust me. Just trust.
On my own I lost my way.
The fog fell
it grew dark and darker still.
I couldn't see through the fog.

ESTHER: You lost.

ROSALIND: I lost.

My name, my work – are they lost too? Am I only
marked by my absence? A woman who reached out and
missed? Whose name history missed out?

What of my work. Does my work still stand up Esther?

ESTHER: Rosalind. Your work is in there. We build on your
work everyday. You can't imagine how much things
have moved on since you – left. This discovery changed
the face of science for us. Unlocking DNA opens up
a whole new set of questions: who are we, why do we
get ill, grow old, die. Every day there's something new,
something big, something momentous. It's going so fast
now – I don't know where to start, where I'm going to
jump on the roller-coaster, where I'm going to go. I just
know I have to be part of it. More than anything I want
to be part of it.

ROSALIND: So the work lives on. The science. Something good comes of this.

JOE: Something good might. Not necessarily.

ESTHER: It is *good* science.

JOE: Yeah. Great.
Zap zap zap. Bob's his own uncle, father, son, child, grandad, grandson. Perfect reproduction. DNA that lives forever. Nothing left to chance. You'll be able to have limitless copies of yourself. Each one exactly the same. You'll be able to walk down the street and see yourself coming towards you. Yourself as you once were. Yourself as you will be. Going on into infinity. You won't have to ask yourself this question about what remains – the thing that remains is you.

ESTHER: Joe likes to be dramatic.

JOE: Don't you patronise me just because I'm not a scientist! I'm still entitled to an opinion. And I'm saying: you haven't thought this through. Some things are questionable. Just because you *can* do something doesn't mean you *must.* And if you accept that we don't know when a bundle of cells, as you put it, becomes a human life, a whole lot of questions are thrown up that you just don't want to answer. You'd rather experiment a bit, win first and make the rules up afterwards. But maybe afterwards will be too late.

ESTHER: The real benefits of this science are huge: we can't stop our research now.

ROSALIND: We must put our trust in the scientists. We must have faith in their faith.

JOE: Not every white coat is a clean one.
You were around in the war. Doesn't human experimentation mean anything to you?

ESTHER: We're not talking about human experimentation. We're not talking about cloning human beings or creating some kind of master race! We're living in the real world, not a comic! This is about medicine. It's about saving lives.

ROSALIND: Wait. Stop. You move too fast for me. Things are moving too fast. A master race, experimenting with human lives – what are you talking about? I can feel the shadow of history in here. Must it all come round again? Is this new science going to be used against people instead of for them? Is this my legacy? Who is being experimented on? Who? Who?

ESTHER: Nobody.

ROSALIND: Joe?

JOE does not reply.

You say this new science is good. Joe says it is not. Who am I to believe?

Scene Seventeen

JOE: (*Grabs the lab-coat he wears as Watson.*) I'm taking us back.

ROSALIND: What?

JOE: Rewind. Let us do that scene again. This time: you watch.

ROSALIND: I don't know what for.

JOE: You have to help us. We can't do this without you.

ROSALIND: Where are we?

JOE: King's again. I'm Watson. I've come to visit Wilkins. Just like last time.

JOE gives ESTHER the papers with Photo 51 amongst them. ESTHER takes Wilkins' jacket again. They get into the same positions as before to play through the Photo 51 scene – Scene Twelve.

JOE / WATSON: You should collaborate, you know, Maurice.

ESTHER / WILKINS: Who with?
With you? But you're not working on DNA any more. Are you? Are you? DNA belongs to us. It's King's problem. That was agreed.

JOE / WATSON: (*Does not answer.*) You should collaborate. The Americans are going to find it if you don't get a move on. It's a race on the final straight.

ESTHER / WILKINS: Rosy says she's leaving. I've been working on this for a very long time. Another month is neither here nor there. I'm not rushing into anything. Once she's gone I'll get down to work. More haste, less speed Jim. Do you know that proverb?

ESTHER / WILKINS is looking at the photo.

JOE / WATSON: You really should collaborate you know.

ESTHER / WILKINS: Will you look here. What's she called this?
(*He turns the photo over to look at the back.*)
Photo 51. This photograph really is very good you know.
It's really quite beautiful.

JOE / WATSON doesn't take the photo – quite demonstratively, he begins to read his paper.

(*Holding out the photo.*) I said it's really quite beautiful.

There's a silence.

JOE / WATSON: (*Still looking at the paper.*) Take it back.
We're not ready.

ESTHER / WILKINS: I said: take a look at this.

JOE gives a cursory glance.

Are you really looking?

*As the present tries to rewrite the past, JOE and ESTHER
override the characters of Watson and Wilkins.*

JOE / WATSON: Take it back. We don't know what we're doing.

ESTHER / WILKINS: Take a look. What do you want to achieve?

JOE / WATSON: Take it back. We can't see where we're going.
Take it back. We need time to think about it.

ESTHER: Take a look. It's the beginning of everything.
A baby who can save a child, a child who doesn't get
sick when you think it must, some parents who don't
have to grieve before their time, children who get to
keep their parents for as long as they should. It's a little
less suffering in the world. Take a look.
(*Pause.*)
Joe, it's so a boy like you doesn't lose his dad when he's
only eleven.
Take a look.

JOE: How can I live with myself if I take it?

ESTHER: How will you live with yourself if you don't?

ROSALIND: You have to look. You have to.
There is no choice now.
What's discovered must remain discovered. Once a fact

is in the world, then we must live with it. We can't go back. Take it. Take it.

ROSALIND turns her back to them again.
Watson and Wilkins dominate the action again. JOE takes the photo, looks, then gives it back.

JOE / WATSON: Hm.

ESTHER / WILKINS goes back to ROSALIND's work-place to put Photo 51 back. JOE / WATSON turns away in his barely suppressed excitement.

Holy Moses! Holy cow! It is a helix! It's definitely a helix.

He makes some quick notes on a newspaper.

ESTHER / WILKINS: It is very good isn't it?

JOE / WATSON: Maurice. (*Shoving the newspaper in his pocket.*) Afraid I have to go now. I'm – playing tennis this evening.

ESTHER / WILKINS: I thought we could have tea in the common room. I could introduce you to the other chaps. We could go to the pub afterwards.

JOE / WATSON: Sorry. I forgot. Prior engagement. You know.

ESTHER / WILKINS: Ah. She's important obviously.

JOE / WATSON: Who?

ESTHER / WILKINS: This woman you're playing tennis with.

JOE / WATSON: Ah. Yes. Yes. She could be.

At the door JOE becomes himself again. He takes off his lab-coat and throws it on the ground and leaves the lab.

ESTHER: (*Taking off the jacket.*) Joe! Joe!

Scene Eighteen

ESTHER: Why did he go? Why didn't he stay?
He doesn't trust me.

ROSALIND: It's – hard to accept we are all responsible.

ESTHER: He doesn't trust me.

ROSALIND: He's unsure of himself.

ESTHER: No responsible scientist is going to put their efforts into cloning babies!
That's not what people want. People just want their own healthy unique child.

ROSALIND: Really, you do think alike.

ESTHER: Huh!

ROSALIND: You will talk. (*Beat.*) But I don't suppose it will be easy.
I have brothers. We did try to talk. But they couldn't understand. Science seemed a little like magic to them, I think.
Although to us it's perfectly clear.

ESTHER: He's gone. He doesn't care.

ROSALIND: He helped us with the experiment, didn't he?

ESTHER: *Helped*? Is it finished then?

ROSALIND: I have to go now.

ESTHER: Not you! Not you too!
What about your work at Birkbeck College? You're moving on to Birkbeck, you said.

ROSALIND: Viruses. It's work on viruses.

ESTHER: Show me.

ROSALIND: There isn't time now.

ESTHER: But isn't it important?

ROSALIND: Of course it's important. But there isn't always time to finish what you set out to do.

ESTHER: So that's it then. Goodbye? Do ghosts say goodbye?

ROSALIND: That's not quite it. We have to go to the end of the story.
(*ESTHER is subdued.*)
I need to finish this. I need you to help me, Esther.
(*Beat.*)
You won't refuse a request for help, will you? You won't say no to a friend?

ESTHER: What do you want me to do?

ROSALIND hands ESTHER a lab-coat.

ESTHER: Who am I?

ROSALIND: A doctor.

ESTHER: A doctor? No, I can't do that. I don't know what to do.

ROSALIND: Of course you can. Put it on. You'll find out what to do.

ESTHER still hasn't taken the coat.

Please. I need to leave now.

ESTHER puts on the lab-coat and stethoscope. Then steps towards ROSALIND, as the doctor.

Scene Nineteen

ESTHER / DOCTOR: Well. Miss Franklin.

ROSALIND: Well. Doctor. This wasn't supposed to happen until much later – in my plan.

ESTHER / DOCTOR: Ah well. Plans and life often go two separate ways, don't they?
Some things are not ours to decide.

ROSALIND: Let's not beat about the bush. There's no room for pleasantries – I have no time for them, I have too much to do.
What is your – assessment.

ESTHER / DOCTOR: It's not good, I'm afraid, Rosalind.

ROSALIND: There must be something else you can do.

ESTHER / DOCTOR: There isn't – really. I'm sorry. We have tried all we know.

ROSALIND: That's it?

ESTHER / DOCTOR: That is the sum of our knowledge.
We've just come to the end of the line with our knowledge.

ROSALIND: But that's absurd.
How little we know.
How little we can do.
How long?

ESTHER / DOCTOR: Not long, I'm afraid.

ROSALIND: Based on?

ESTHER / DOCTOR: Previous experience.

ROSALIND: There can be exceptions.

ESTHER / DOCTOR: Size of tumour. Situation of tumour. Secondary growths. Do you need any more evidence?

ROSALIND: I don't want evidence. I want hope. I want time.

ESTHER / DOCTOR: Rosalind.
You are lucky. Look on it as being lucky. You have a little time to prepare yourself for what is coming.

ROSALIND: I'm not interested in the mechanics of this. I've got too much to do.

ESTHER / DOCTOR: Is your soul ready?

ROSALIND: My soul! Don't be absurd. I'm a scientist. I want time now. My work isn't finished. It isn't ready.

ESTHER / DOCTOR: We are not made to live forever.

ROSALIND: I haven't said I want forever. I haven't asked for that. I have work that must carry on. I just need to make plans.

ESTHER / DOCTOR: Make your plans. Make them. But in my experience, it is easier for us to go with some kind of faith. Do you not have faith?

ROSALIND: Of course I have faith! But I don't accept your definition of faith – a life after death! For me faith is the belief that through dedication to our work we can come closer to improving the lot of mankind. Only that matters. I have workers who need to carry on. The work must carry on!

ROSALIND breaks away and relaxes, visibly. ESTHER is released from playing the doctor, takes off the coat.

Thank you.

ESTHER: So short. Your life was so short.

ROSALIND: Science goes on. My work goes on. I know that now.

ESTHER: You've finished with me. Shall I go now?

ROSALIND: Go? You've hardly started. This is your space now.

ESTHER: But what am I supposed to do?

ROSALIND: You *know* what you want to do.

ESTHER: I want to be useful, my work to be of use. I want to make Joe see it with his own eyes: that research is about saving lives.

ROSALIND: So that's your challenge: there's your mountain. Which path are you going to take?

ESTHER: I don't know. I can't see it yet. What should I do? I have to look at everything first. There's so much. I shall have to think before I make a decision. About what kind of work I do and *how* I do it. It feels like such a responsibility. It's all down to me.

ROSALIND: It is down to you.
But you're here because you're not afraid to take a risk, because you followed your intuition, because you're a scientist. Sometimes it takes bravery to be a scientist. You have to have the courage to strike out with an idea that's right and good and stick with it. In spite of what anyone else might think.
But you're not on your own. You have to remember that. So many contribute to the journey in science. So many. And when you get to work with a good team, you'll see – it's the most satisfying thing in the world.
We were a good team today. I couldn't have done my experiment without you.

ESTHER: Thank you, Rosalind. I'll finish that then.

As they cross each other ROSALIND places her hand very briefly on ESTHER's arm in a gesture of farewell. ESTHER sits at her lap-top to finish the job application. ROSALIND is at her desk. The women are in separate pools of light.

ROSALIND: It's never finished.
We scrape around to leave a mark on the earth, some sign we have been here: a child, our name, our work – but it must all move on, time sweeps away everything. It will make it easier for me to know there's someone here working away. That it's not all wasted.
I'm glad you're here.

The lights fade.

Printed in the USA
CPSIA information can be obtained
at www.ICGtesting.com
LVHW020954171024
794056LV00004B/1122